F. SCOTT FITZGERALD
Writer of the Jazz Age

F. SCOTT FITZGERALD
Writer of the Jazz Age

Virginia Brackett

MORGAN
REYNOLDS
Publishers, Inc.

620 South Elm Street, Suite 223
Greensboro, North Carolina   27406
http://www.morganreynolds.com

F. SCOTT FITZGERALD: WRITER OF THE JAZZ AGE

Copyright © 2002 by Virginia Brackett

Library of Congress Cataloging-in-Publication Data

Brackett, Virginia.
    F. Scott Fitzgerald : writer of the Jazz Age / Virginia Brackett.-- 1st ed.
      p. cm.
    Includes bibliographical references (p.) and index.
    Summary: Describes the life and career of the twentieth-century American author
  whose works include "The Great Gatsby" and "This Side of Paradise."
    ISBN 1-883846-90-0 (lib. bdg.)
      1. Fitzgerald, F. Scott (Francis Scott), 1896-1940--Juvenile literature. 2. Authors,
  American--20th century--Biography--Juvenile literature. [1. Fitzgerald, F. Scott (Francis
  Scott), 1896-1940. 2. Authors, American.] I. Title.

  PS3511.I9 Z5588 2002
  813'.52--dc21
  [B]
                                                                    2001056284

Printed in the United States of America
First Edition

For Shandra, who reads Fitzgerald

Contents

F. Scott Fitzgerald
(Library of Congress)

Chapter One

Born to Write

By 1920, World War I was over. While world-wide strife wound down, the United States of America began to wind up. During the next decade, nicknamed the "Roaring Twenties," many Americans would enjoy a long-awaited celebration. Happy days had at last arrived, and the urge to reject traditions for new fads was strong.

Prohibition laws, passed in 1920, forbade the production and sale of liquor. But this move only fueled the drive to defy authority. Who could celebrate without alcohol? Illegal "bootlegged" gin and corn liquor "mills" were soon easily available, and "gangsters," such as Chicago's infamous Al Capone, made millions through its distribution and sale. Enterprising individuals concocted their own liquor at home, and the phrase "bath tub gin" became part of the vocabulary. That vocabulary also included terms such as "Speak Easy," and "joint," nicknames for bars where people could obtain illegal liquor.

While indulging their thirsts, party-goers also frol-
icked to a new musical sound, known as "jazz." With
wild drum beats and blasting horns, jazz bands whipped
people into a dancing frenzy. Even the fashions
screamed "party," as young women "bobbed" their hair,
cutting it short for easy care, and wore short, baggy
sequined dresses with fringe that swirled as they twirled.

During this decade a young American writer named
F. Scott Fitzgerald immortalized these "flappers," as the
dancers were called, in his 1920 collection of stories,
Flappers and Philosophers. His next story collection in
1922, *Tales of the Jazz Age*, helped to name an era
characterized for its confusion of quick wealth with
personal satisfaction. It was a time that destroyed the
weak and those with a craving for power and money.
Scott created the representative character of the era
with his mysterious Jay Gatsby, who makes a fortune
illegally in order to win the love of a rich girl. In the
end, Scott himself became a victim of the Jazz Age,
caught up in a lifestyle he could never escape.

Born September 24, 1896, in St. Paul, Minnesota,
Francis Scott Key Fitzgerald later claimed he knew
from childhood that he would write. In part, he credited
his interest in stories to his mother, Mollie. But even
Mollie could not have predicted the impression her son
would make on the writing world.

Scott's parents had unspectacular backgrounds.
Mollie McQuillan grew up a respected, well-to-do Catholic in St. Paul. Her father, a poor Irish immigrant in

1843, died a wealthy man in 1877. He had accumulated more than $200,000 and owned a group of wholesale food businesses worth millions. Mollie grew up financially secure, but the McQuillans were not considered "fashionable." A shy girl, Mollie loved to read. Scott would inherit his mother's passion for literature, but not her personality. He gained his handsome face and charming manner from his father, Edward Fitzgerald.

Mollie always wanted to marry, but few men found her interesting. When she was almost thirty years old, she agreed to marry Edward, a suitor of several years. A fine looking man, but with few prospects for a successful future, Edward came from Chicago, where he managed a furniture business. His one qualification was that he adored Mollie. Following their February 1890 wedding, he wrote to his brother, "I have drawn a prize in a wife."

The Fitzgeralds remained in St. Paul, where Mollie quickly had two daughters. Then, during Mollie's third pregnancy, both girls became ill and died. Grief stricken, Mollie and Edward took comfort in the birth of Francis Scott—later shortened to Scott. Weighing a healthy ten pounds, the baby was named for his famous ancestor, Francis Scott Key, writer of the "Star Spangled Banner." From the start, Mollie made sure that Scott believed in his special position in the world. She constantly praised her son, repeatedly telling him that he could be a great man. More than anyone, Scott's doting mother helped shape his determined, flashy personality.

Mollie rarely spoke to her son about the pain of losing her daughters. She used her frequent prayer visits to the Catholic church to ease her pain. When Scott learned about the two sisters he would never know, the information affected him in an odd way. He later explained that, although he was not sure why, after learning of those deaths, he "started then to be a writer."

When Scott was about eighteen months old, Edward's business failed, and the Fitzgeralds moved. Edward hoped to succeed as a Procter & Gamble salesman in Buffalo, New York. In 1901, when Scott was five years old, Edward again relocated the family, this time to Syracuse, New York. That same year Scott's younger sister Annabel was born. The Fitzgeralds returned to Buffalo in 1903. Despite the moves, Scott had a normal childhood and later retained vivid memories of those New York years.

Once, at age six, Scott ran away from home on the Fourth of July. He spent the day in a pear orchard with a friend. When he returned home he received a spanking from his father, then sat out on the porch to watch fireworks. The next day he walked with his father into town. Scott recalled carrying his own walking cane and having his shoes shined, like his father. He remembered spending many hours with his friends. The boys tied strings around their toes at night when they went to bed, dangling the strings out the window. In the morning, the one who got up first pulled the strings to awaken the other boys.

From the beginning, Scott Fitzgerald's mother wanted her son to feel that he was special. *(Library of Congress)*

Scott and his best friend, Hamilton Wende, both loved drama. They regularly attended Saturday plays by Buffalo's summer troupe. After watching a play the boys hurried home to act it out. Scott often memorized many of the actors' speeches. The only disagreement Scott had with Hamilton was over sports. Hamilton tried out for school teams, but Scott wanted to read in the library instead. His attitude toward sports would soon change, and he joined the teams.

Mollie dressed Scott with a great deal of care. She wanted him to make a good impression at social gatherings. She often explained to Hamilton that her son needed to meet children in addition to him. Mollie constantly encouraged Scott to attract as much attention, in a mannerly way, as possible. She took Scott with her to Mass as part of his social training. When Scott was nine, Mollie urged Edward to move the family to a better neighborhood, for Scott's benefit.

Small-boned with blond hair and his mother's large eyes, Scott's feminine appearance often singled him out for teasing. He took the teasing well and never hesitated to speak up in class or with his friends. He sometimes rebelled against school work, although he loved to read. *Ivanhoe*, Sir Walter Scott's tale of knights, heroes, and damsels-in-distress, was one of Scott's favorite novels. He also loved poetry that told gruesome or adventurous tales, such as Edgar Allen Poe's "The Raven."

By 1908, Scott began playing basketball and noticing girls. He had a crush on a girl named Kiddy Williams whom he wrote about in the "Thought Book" kept under his bed. He noted that although he was "third in her affections," he would one day "gain first place."

The Fitzgeralds's happy life was interrupted in March when Edward again lost his job. Scott later wrote about the incident. When his mother answered his father's phone call delivering the news, he knew that something terrible had happened. He also feared that they would again be short of money. Mollie had given him a quarter to go swimming, and he handed it back. Then he prayed, "Dear God, don't let us go to the poorhouse." While he loved his father and admired his looks and style, Scott eventually learned that Edward Fitzgerald lacked ambition. Insufficient ambition would never be a problem for Scott.

The Fitzgeralds returned to St. Paul and to Mollie's family, who had enough money to ease the strain within the family. They lived for a time in Grandmother McQuillan's house, and Scott began school at the St. Paul Academy. One of the teachers who came to know him well was C.N.B. Wheeler. Wheeler taught English and history and served as the school's coach. He encouraged Scott to record his stories. He noted that, while not a good student, Scott showed great promise in writing and helped to create small "playlets" for his class. Because Scott loved drama, Mr. Wheeler predicted he would become an actor. Scott was not particularly popular, and Mr. Wheeler credited Scott's writings as the cause. Occasionally he wrote about the other children, sometimes with too much honesty.

Scott did have a few close friends at school. He enjoyed sports, and although strong for his size, he was just too small to compete in football. That did not stop him from trying. He tackled the biggest members of opposing teams, occasionally injuring himself. According to Scott's friends he enjoyed acting the injured hero. Creative writing remained his favorite activity though. By 1909, during his second year at St. Paul, his work appeared in the school magazine.

Life at home was not as much fun. In addition to his parents and grandmother, Scott lived with two maiden aunts who, dressed in black, attended daily Mass and expected the family to attend as well. Mollie also dressed in black and lost herself in reading and making daily trips to the library. Edward's interest in his family faded. The McQuillans were not as wealthy as when Grandfather McQuillan had been alive, and Edward's lack of drive did not suit Grandmother or the aunts. Scott understood the power of money, and he enjoyed watching the men in the stables across from his house washing the carriages of his rich neighbors. Mollie remained determined that Scott would not suffer due to his father's failures. Aware of the importance of social connections, she enrolled Scott in a dancing class in 1909. Unlike other boys in the class who wore "common" blue suits, Scott always dressed in formal black.

Scott's friends enjoyed hiking, bicycling, and roller

The Fitzgeralds moved into Mollie's family home in St. Paul.
(Library of Congress)

skating. They went on winter sleigh rides and then drank hot chocolate, followed by dancing. Girls liked Scott, and he liked them. His relationships with boys did not develop as easily. He had to prove himself worthy of their friendships and earned their favor by thinking up exciting activities. Soon Scott was receiving plenty of invitations, even though his parents did not mingle with his friends' parents. Residents of St. Paul appreciated good breeding, which both Edward and Mollie had, but they also expected a man to work, to do something of note. Edward Fitzgerald would never be that type of man. Scott's love for his father remained strong, but his respect dwindled.

Scott would describe many of his early adventures later in highly romantic stories. He became an idealist, imagining the best of everyone and supposing life would give him its best. In a series called the "Basil stories," Scott modeled the hero, Basil Duke Lee, on himself. One story tells of Basil's crush on a girl whose affection he loses to a more "manly" boy. Scott's self-perception as a sensitive, intellectual individual represented an attitude that would carry over into adulthood.

In another of the stories, Basil expressed enthusiasm about leaving his Midwest home for an East coast boarding school. In 1911, Scott himself would enroll in Newman, a school outside Hackensack, New Jersey. A small institution that accepted only sixty applicants from well-to-do Catholic families, Newman prepared its students for college. Scott evaluated his prospects as he enrolled in Newman. He wrote that he considered himself "fortunate" and "capable of expansion," a capability that he based upon his "superior mentality." He added that, "I must excell [sic], even in the eyes of others," and "I was sure that I exercised a subtle fascination over women." He describes himself as "vain" but also "talented, ingenuous and quick to learn." Scott did balance this positive list with a few negatives, including his "desire to influence" others, at times "for evil." He also described himself as sometimes selfish, "cold" and "capable of being cruel," adding that he may have "lacked a sense of honor." Whatever his shortcomings, Scott believed that underneath all of his personality traits "lay a sense of infinite possibilities."

Scott cut classes and the required Catholic masses during his first semester at Newman. He also became less conceited, as his classmates would not put up with his superior attitude. He made close friends and occasionally visited with relatives. One cousin, Cecilia Taylor, was sixteen years older than Scott and had invited him as a child to be a "ribbon holder" in her wedding. Scott's favorite relative, Cecilia would be the model for the character Clara in his first novel, *This Side of Paradise*. By his second term at Newman his grades began to improve, and he continued to play sports.

During summers between school terms, Scott discovered that the St. Paul girls found his Newman-trained manners attractive. Their praise soon spoiled him and the St. Paul boys ignored him. After reading a book by

Owen Johnson called *Stover at Yale*, Scott decided that he wanted to become a football hero. He practiced tackling a dummy in his backyard and took part in football games upon returning to school. At five feet six inches and 130 pounds, Scott could move quickly, but his short legs made him appear awkward as he charged down the field.

By his sixth semester at Newman, Scott became confident of his writing talent when the *Newman News* published three of his stories. While many of Scott's fellow students found him too preoccupied with his own appearance and talents, teachers liked Scott. They forgave his frequent tardiness once he struck up conversations with them that often had nothing to do with the day's lessons. No one was surprised when, during a rehearsal of William Shakespeare's *The Taming of the Shrew*, Scott suggested ways to improve Shakespeare's lines. He became a favorite of Elizabeth Magoffin. She was the director of the Elizabethan Drama Club, that was named after her. That group performed at the local YMCA, often for charitable causes. Scott wrote a play, *The Coward*, that was given two performances, one at the YMCA, and another at a local yacht club.

Rather than do his lessons, Scott read constantly and said that the only subjects that caught his interest were geometry and John Milton's poetry. During evenings he enjoyed smoking with a friend beside Newman's baseball diamond. They gossiped about classmates and made jokes about their futures.

Scott was determined to attend Princeton University. He claimed as his reason the fact that Princeton had lost its most recent football game to Yale. Scott wrote that the game seemed like a child's story, in which the big unlikable animals defeat the smaller, more likeable ones. He saw the Princeton men "as slender and keen and romantic, and the Yale men as "brawny and brutal and powerful." Scott had chosen the self-image he would strive to retain for life as a "Princeton Man."

Chapter Two

Writing, College, and Romance

At age sixteen, Scott took the college admittance exams. He later confessed that he cheated, something he would always regret. While he passed the exams, his grades during his final semester at Newman were too low for him to gain entrance to Princeton. During August of 1913, he prepared for make-up exams in various courses, hoping to raise his grades. He did not succeed and decided to take advantage of the procedure allowed to Princeton applicants who had "borderline" scores. They could travel to the university in New Jersey, appear before a committee, and argue their case. Supposedly during his appearance, Scott told the committee members that it was his birthday and they should not turn him down. Whatever he said, it proved convincing. On September 24, 1913, his seventeenth birthday, he sent Mollie a telegram reading, "ADMITTED SEND FOOTBALL PADS AND SHOES IMMEDIATELY PLEASE WAIT TRUNK."

Unfortunately, Scott was too small to do well on the football field. He quickly found other things to enjoy at Princeton. He wrote of being enthralled by the upperclassmen who paraded about the campus. At the group's head was the football captain, a Princeton senior of high standing. Like the other freshmen, Scott worshipped from a distance, because upperclassmen did not mix with lowerclassmen. His more formal worship as a Catholic churchgoer, however, diminished. Scott had little use for religious doctrine.

Scott willingly complied with the requirements for freshmen; sophomores could command them to dance, and they could not smoke pipes on campus or tread on the grass. All freshmen had to wear pants without cuffs, shirts with stiff collars, black skullcaps and garters that supported their dark socks. Eager to fit in, Scott imitated his classmates' actions. He shared his housing, nicknamed "The Morgue," with nine freshmen, several of whom had come from Newman. Scott joined in the card games, pillow fights, and serious arguments regarding the future of American society. He became known as a prankster who enjoyed causing "blackouts" in the house. He had discovered that the gas lights would all go out, leaving the house dark, if he blew into the gas jet on the house's third floor.

Scott had a clear sense of himself as a writer and was not shy about publicizing his high regard for his own talent. In some early letters from Newman and Princeton, he followed his signature with the notation "playwright."

He had also begun to enjoy drinking. Because alcohol was prohibited on campus, he joined groups on trips to bars along Nassau Street, close to Princeton.

Rather than focusing on studies, Scott concentrated on getting published in the *Tiger*, a small newspaper that printed humorous items. He submitted piece after piece, even sneaking one into a book that belonged to the editor. Weakening under the piles of submissions from Scott, the editor of the *Tiger* did print two of his "squibs," or funny remarks. Scott also fixated on having an original work produced by the Triangle Club, a Princeton playhouse that presented musicals. During his first semester he submitted some lyrics, but works by upperclassmen were chosen for the next musical. He immersed himself in extra-curricular activities, hardly bothering to attend class. When he went home for Christmas, he had taken the maximum number of absences allowed, having cut class forty-nine times.

Scott especially liked the train rides home during school breaks and the exciting crowds in Chicago's Union Station, where he would change trains for St. Paul. Always attentive to others' social plans, he listened to young people discuss whose holiday parties they would attend. He also livened the sometimes dull atmosphere of St. Paul by asking young women flattering questions, such as "What sort of a heroine would you like to be?" He wanted to give his "audience" the idea that he could be published at any moment.

When he returned to Princeton, Scott failed three of

his midterm exams and barely passed four, just managing to remain enrolled. He immediately began work on a script for a contest held by the Triangle Club. Only two submissions were still under consideration by the end of April, one of which belonged to Scott. In May Scott was proclaimed the contest winner, mainly because the lyrics to his songs were judged so original. He later explained that he had studied the work of well-known musical composers Gilbert and Sullivan, along with the snappy dialogue of British writer Oscar Wilde.

Scott began a pattern of befriending other aspiring writers that would continue throughout his lifetime. In his second semester, Scott met John Peale Bishop, a man who would later become an accomplished poet and novelist. Bishop later wrote about their first meeting. He said the two young men discussed books, the few that he had read, the fewer that Scott read, and the large number that Scott claimed he had read. In actuality, Bishop was quite well read and, due to childhood illness, much older than Scott when he began classes at Princeton. At twenty-one, he had a sophisticated air that many of the students did not like, but it fascinated Scott. Peale provided the basis for a character in *This Side of Paradise* named Thomas Parke d'Invilliers.

In the summer of 1914, Scott stayed in St. Paul. He remained too busy to pay much attention to the activities in Europe that would soon erupt into World War I. He socialized when possible and continued working out plots and lyrics for the Triangle Club. He also focused on his third play for the Elizabethan Dramatic Club, *Assorted Spirits*, another hit with its audiences. While the Germans' movements toward Paris interested Scott, the chance of the United States becoming involved in the European war seemed remote.

When Scott returned to Princeton in the fall of 1914, his main concern was that he would not be allowed to act in the Triangle Club productions. Although he had improved his grades, they did not qualify him to travel with the group, so he helped with directing and rewriting. Living alone during that second year, he continued to skip classes. In chemistry class he often wrote verse, but he did become interested in the Romantic poets in English class. This was partly due to the student gatherings at the professor's home where they read poetry aloud while drinking rum-spiked tea.

During his second Princeton Christmas break, Scott began his first serious romance. In January of 1915 he met a young woman from a wealthy and socially prominent family. Ginerva King came from Lake Forest, outside of Chicago. She and Scott met at a party. When he returned to Princeton, Scott wrote often to Ginerva and referred to her in letters to others. He worried about his rivals for her affections back in Lake Forest. He invited her to the sophomore prom, and when she declined he accepted her refusal gracefully. They agreed to meet the following summer.

In that spring of 1915 Scott became acquainted with another Princeton writer named Edmund Wilson. The two formed a friendship that lasted all of Scott's life. Wilson, nicknamed "Bunny," edited the *Nassau Literary Magazine* and published Scott's one-act play, *Shadow Laurels,* as well as a short story called "The Ordeal." The two friends were opposites in many ways. Wilson was a logical intellectual with few social skills, while Scott was a man of imagination who loved high society. After graduating, Wilson became one of America's most influential men of letters. He published novels and became editor of the magazines *Vanity Fair* and the *New Republic.* Wilson would eventually serve as the literary critic for the *New Yorker* where he would review Scott's fiction.

Throughout his Princeton years, Scott remained dedicated to writing about the social scene. He continued to disregard Europe's escalating war. He used his letters to discuss ideas that would appear in his short stories. A 1915 letter to his sister Annabel serves as a good example. He offered Annabel advice, such as "In your conversation always affect a complete frankness but really be only as frank as you wish to be. Never try to give a boy the affect that you're popular."

Years later Scott added a note at the top of that letter identifying it as the basis for one of his most popular short stories, "Bernice Bobs Her Hair," that appeared in the *Saturday Evening Post* in 1920. The story was an early example of one of his consistent themes: the competition among individuals for social success, and the determination of the hero of the story to "win" despite the odds. In that particular plot, Bernice, a plain-faced teenaged girl with beautiful long hair, visits her lovely, sophisticated teenaged cousin, Marjorie. Marjorie convinces Bernice to mimic her and to act the role of a lively snob in order to attract boys. As part of her role playing, Bernice promises to cut her hair, inviting the popular crowd to watch. Marjorie knows that Bernice's plain features will not be flattered by such a "bob," but Bernice believes Marjorie's empty promise that the cut will bring with it instant popularity. Of course, it does not, and Marjorie glories in having tricked her cousin. Bernice gains revenge, however, when she snips off Marjorie's own golden braids while she sleeps. It was a perfect example of a satisfying Fitzgerald plot in which the underdog triumphs over social adversity.

Scott would base such stories on many of his own relationships and experiences. In June of 1915 he met Ginerva in New York City for their long-planned date. They watched a stage performance and then had dinner in a restaurant. Scott still felt he had a chance to win Ginerva's devotion, despite the wide differences in their families' social status. On his way home to St. Paul he stopped in Chicago to see Ginerva again, then visited a friend in Wyoming during July and August. Hardly the outdoor type, Scott did not care for the ranch where he stayed, but he did not want to look like a sissy. Talk that summer centered on girls and school, but occasionally turned to events in Europe.

He had to return to Princeton early for tutoring. He

Edmund Wilson became a friend of Fitzgerald's at Princeton. Later, he would become an influential editor who was often critical of Fitzgerald's work. *(Library of Congress)*

continued to write for the *Nassau Literary Magazine* and the *Tiger*. He still longed to be a football hero and annoyed some of his classmates with his false compliments and childish complaints about class work. In November he contracted malaria, not an uncommon disease at Princeton, and using illness as an excuse, withdrew from classes. He received a rude shock when he returned the following February of 1916 to discover that he would have to repeat his junior year. He asked the Dean of Princeton to write a note to the effect that he withdrew voluntarily. Then Scott returned to St. Paul to wait for fall classes to begin.

During the summer of 1916 he again visited Ginerva. At a party he overheard a guest say that "poor boys shouldn't think of marrying rich girls." When Scott returned to Princeton in the fall of 1916, his romance with Ginerva was over. While she visited him for the November Princeton-Yale football game, she only spent a short time with him. She met another boy. Scott continued to write to her, but gave up when he received no response. He did not turn to prayer for help, as he had so many years ago when his father lost his job. Instead, he wrote furiously. In his next story appearing in the *Nassau Lit*, the hero was an author who won the girl he loved, but then lost the ability to write. This story continued Scott's method of using his own life, and the lives of those close to him, as story material. He learned an important lesson. He could turn personal loss into art.

Chapter Three

Zelda

By spring of 1917, the threat of war touched Princeton. Germany had taken possession of much territory in Europe, and the Allies had reacted strongly during 1916 to try to recover some ground. The United States had remained neutral, and in 1916 President Woodrow Wilson attempted to help negotiate a peace treaty. His effort failed, and Germany declared an all-out attack on all ship traffic. Wilson dropped his peacemaking attempts and made it clear that the United States sided with Britain and France. On April 6, 1917, the United States declared war against Germany.

About that time, Scott traveled to New York City to visit Edmund Wilson, who was working as a reporter. After the two friends discussed war and literature, Scott returned to Princeton determined to become a poet. He knew the coming war was going to change his life. Scott later wrote, "I had read somewhere that every great poet had written great poetry before he was twenty-one. I had only a year and, besides, war was impending. I must publish a startling book before I was engulfed."

In August of 1917 Scott received a letter from Cyril Sigourney Webster Fay, who had become headmaster of the Newman School following Scott's graduation. Fay knew that Scott no longer attended Mass or considered the Catholic Church an important part of his life. He hoped to take Scott with him on a religious mission to Russia, where he planned to spark interest in the Catholic Church and also to rekindle Scott's religious faith. Father Fay corresponded with Scott not only about the trip, but also about his writing. He became Scott's supporter and informal literary critic.

When the fall semester began in 1917, Scott knew he would not graduate with his class. School work did not appeal to him, and his rejection of the Catholic faith was now almost complete. Father Fay continued to correspond with Scott, as well as with Shane Leslie, a young Irish writer who spent time in the United States. Fay hoped that Leslie could bring Scott back to his faith, and the two discussed Catholicism in his presence. The discussions did little to change Scott's mind.

Scott did decide to travel to Russia with Fay. He did not care about the religious mission, but was excited about visiting Russia, which was in the middle of a revolution. While waiting for the trip, Scott submitted some poems for publication. One was accepted by a magazine called *Poet Lore*, although the poem would never be printed. When the Russia trip was canceled because of the war, Scott decided to follow a new plan. He would join the army, travel as a soldier, maybe fight in the war, and collect material to write about. By the end of October, 1917, Scott had been given a commission as a second lieutenant and received his assignment to Ft. Leavenworth, Kansas.

Scott arrived in Kansas just in time for a bitter winter. As he went through three months of officer training he also worked on his first novel. He sent drafts to Father Fay, who praised the book that Scott was calling *The Romantic Egoist*. Fay wrote that he found the story to be "first rate stuff." He would eventually send it to Shane Leslie, who added his positive comments. Father Fay served as the model for the character in the novel named Father Darcy. Scott would also dedicate the novel to Fay, soon to be promoted in the Church to a Monsignor. Typical of his sincere but careless attitude, Scott misspelled Fay's name in the dedication.

John Peale Bishop also corresponded with Scott during his training to be an infantry officer. Like Scott, Bishop wanted to be involved in real battle. Having recently published a collection of poetry, Bishop also offered to review Scott's novel. He found it somewhat ordinary, but told Scott that it did have a universal appeal. Scott must have felt torn about his writing. In November he received a letter from Shane Leslie that said, "I wish you would stick to your idea of a book of poems." However, Scott persisted with the novel, and in March 1918, he sent the completed manuscript to Leslie.

Leslie proofread it and sent it to a publishing company called Scribners. He requested that even if they did not want to publish the manuscript they keep it for a while. He wanted Scott to be able to depart for Europe feeling he had a future as a novelist.

Scott thought he was on his way to the war in Europe. Instead, he was sent to Kentucky for his first assignment with the Forty-fifth Infantry Regiment. In mid-April the Regiment relocated, first to Georgia, and later to Camp Sheridan, Alabama. The Regiment became part of the newly-formed Ninth Division, which was preparing to ship out to Europe. As a first lieutenant, Scott gained a reputation for not following orders and for sometimes abusing the men in his command.

During preparations and training, Scott traveled into nearby Montgomery, where he observed the Southern culture with interest. He enjoyed the romantic atmosphere of a place that seemed to have changed little over time. Black men herded cattle down the main streets each morning, and wealthy white socialites could be seen traveling from one event to another. Scott was also lonely, and news of Ginerva's upcoming marriage only made him feel more lost and neglected. He wrote to Fay of his loneliness and Fay suggested that he retain his fear of God as protection. Scott would soon find a different outlet for his feelings.

In July of 1918 Scott attended a dance at the local country club. The wealthy families of Montgomery often invited the young officers stationed nearby to attend social functions. At this party Scott met a recent high school graduate named Zelda Sayre. Born on July 24, 1900, to parents both in their forties, Zelda had been named after a gypsy queen in a novel. Although the Sayres' sixth child, she was, like Scott, her mother's pampered favorite. Minnie Sayre nursed Zelda until she was four years old, encouraged Zelda's irrepressible energy, and excused her faults.

Zelda was a Montgomery debutante when Scott met her. The debutantes, making their formal "debut" into society, attended many large parties, specifically to search for a husband. A few months short of her eighteenth birthday, Zelda enchanted Scott with her beautiful complexion and honey-colored hair. One friend commented on the fact that the two already looked like a couple. They even resembled each other with their pale skin, slender builds, and blond hair. Scott was impressed by Zelda's looks, as well as her attitude. Like Scott, Zelda craved excitement.

Following the dance, Scott visited Zelda and her father, who was a judge. Judge Anthony Sayre approved of the young army officer. Scott shared his plans to become a writer with Zelda and his confidence that he would soon be famous. The pair became the center of attention at each of the many social events they attended. Scott seemed to have found his soul mate.

Scribners returned Scott's novel manuscript in August with praise and suggestions for improvement. By October he had revised the manuscript and resubmitted it. He was disappointed when it came back again with a final rejection. The good news was that Scott's writing had impressed an editor named Maxwell Perkins, who would remember the young writer.

Scott continued his correspondence with Bishop, who was on the European war front. Desperately hoping to join the fighting, Scott watched with disappointment as the war seemed to be winding down. He marched onto a ship due to depart in late October, only to be ordered off again. The Armistice, or peace agreement, had been signed. When Scott's regiment prepared to return to Washington D.C., he could not be located. One story relates that when Scott's men arrived, they found him waiting at the railroad station with one girl on each knee. He claimed to have taken over a private train, pretending that he carried secret papers for President Woodrow Wilson.

Scott remained in the service for a short time after the war serving as personal aide to the commander of the Seventeenth Infantry Brigade. Despite falling off his horse during a parade and generally misbehaving, Scott's charm kept him out of trouble. He had no intention, however, of remaining in the army. His future would contain fame and fortune and, hopefully, Zelda Sayre.

Scott visited Zelda as often as possible. They liked to discuss poetry while sipping tea on her porch. They also drank gin together and kissed in the back rows of the local theater. When Zelda shared her diary with

When Scott met Zelda Sayre in Montgomery, Alabama, in 1918, she was a debutante with a long line of suitors. *(Library of Congress)*

Scott, he was so impressed with her writing and thoughts that he would later use many of her phrases in his stories. Zelda knew how to keep Scott interested. Although she declared her love for Scott, she continued to date others.

In January, 1919, Scott learned that Monsignor Fay had suddenly died. In his typical romantic view, he wrote to Shane Leslie that he felt in some way Fay's mantle had fallen on his shoulders. He felt responsible to "some day recreate an atmosphere of him."

By February, Scott had been discharged from the service. He asked Zelda to marry him, but she refused. She said she could not marry a man who she was not sure could support her in the lifestyle she wanted to live. She wanted to escape Montgomery and travel and live in exciting places.

Scott decided to move to New York and pursue his fortune as a writer. He found a room and began searching for a job as a reporter or editor. Instead, he found himself writing ads for street cars at an advertising agency.

Meanwhile, Scott worried about Zelda back in Montgomery. He knew she was popular and had many suitors interested in marrying her. Aviators from the nearby Camp Taylor flew over her house to impress her. Five football players formed a group to honor Zelda. Its "initiation" consisted of trips to Zelda's home. Zelda tried to ease Scott's worries by writing, "Sweetheart, please don't worry about me . . . You know I am all yours and love you with all my heart." Scott sent a telegram that read, in part, "EVERYTHING IS POSSIBLE I AM IN THE LAND OF AMBITION AND SUCCESS AND MY ONLY HOPE AND FAITH IS THAT MY DARLING HEART WILL BE WITH ME SOON."

Scott's boss at the advertising agency liked his work and predicted a long future for him with the company. This was not what Scott envisioned for himself, however. He continued to work on stories, poems, and plays. When they were rejected, he sent them out again and began work on new pieces. He also wrote to Zelda's parents expressing his intentions of marriage.

By March of 1919 Zelda was tired of waiting. She wrote to Scott that women "love to fancy themselves suffering." According to Zelda, such silly romantic attitudes were responsible for much of what was wrong with men. It was men who needed to be more miserable "for the improvement of things in general." Scott would place Zelda's words almost verbatim in the mouth of his character Rosalind in *This Side of Paradise*, his new title for the novel he was currently revising again.

When he could no longer stand the separation, Scott traveled to Montgomery. He wanted to convince Zelda to accept a formal engagement. She refused. Back in New York he spent part of his free time drinking at the Princeton and Yale Club. Once, when he threatened to jump from a window of the club, he was told to go ahead, that the French-designed windows were perfect for such an activity. He complained about his low salary, remarking that he spent his entire $20 week's wages on lingerie for Zelda. He became annoyed when a friend suggested that he try to live within his income.

Scott enjoyed looking at apartments that he could not afford, but was insulted when one landlady told him he could bring women into the apartment. He wrote to Zelda, telling her he now understood why in the old stories "they locked princesses in towers." Zelda responded in April that Scott had written that same line in several recent letters. She ended by expressing her love, but added, "if it's going to be so much longer, we just *can't* keep up this frantic letter writing." The very next day Scott visited Montgomery, then returned to New York an emotional wreck. He asked his employer to fire him, but his boss told him to go home and rest.

Zelda's attitude toward Scott seemed both hopeful and distant, depending on the tone of her letters. After strolling through a graveyard, one of her favorite activities, Zelda wrote to Scott that she wondered how people would remember her. Even at her young age, and despite her foolish activities, Zelda often expressed a longing for immortality. She concluded by telling Scott "Old death is so beautiful—so very beautiful—We will die together I know—Sweetheart." While Scott wanted to feel encouraged, he knew that she continued to see other "sweethearts" in Montgomery.

Chapter Four

Birth of a Professional

Scott continued his active night life. During one incident on May Day of 1919, he and a friend named Porter Gillespie visited a restaurant following a fraternity party. A food fight began and Scott was kicked out of the restaurant. Scott kept trying to sneak back in by crawling through the door as new guests entered. Eventually, Scott and Porter went from hotel bar to hotel bar trying to buy champagne. At one bar they stole the "In" and "Out" signs from the coat check room. Each fastened one to their lapels and introduced themselves to others as "Mr. In" and "Mr. Out." Scott would later base a short story called "May Day" on that incident. This was during a time of political upheaval in the country, with political riots in New York City and many people advocating a socialist government. However, only later would Scott see the seriousness of those times. Then he recalled being "haunted" by his real life, "my drab room . . . my shabby suits, my poverty, and love."

Scott made more frantic visits to Montgomery to plead with Zelda to marry him. In June she decided to end their relationship. While she told Scott that she loved him, she said he lived a dull lifestyle that did not appeal to her. Zelda continued attending parties and dances, while Scott was devastated. He told a friend that if he could not marry Zelda, he would never marry at all. He quit his job and went on a drinking binge. Early in July he felt happier when a well-known magazine, the *Smart Set*, bought one of his stories. This news followed 121 rejections. The story was one that had already appeared in the *Nassau Lit*, and Scott became glum again because he had not sold any new material.

At age twenty-two Scott decided to move home to St. Paul to work on his novel. His parents had always been supportive and had sent him money, although not enough to satisfy Scott. Mollie had hoped that Scott would make a career of the military, while Edward hoped he would go into business. Now they agreed to support him for a limited time as he worked on his novel.

Scott went to work to complete *This Side of Paradise* with a self-discipline he had never shown before. He wrote for hours, stopping only to eat the food Mollie brought to his room. She and Edward left him alone to work, intercepting phone calls and preventing other interruptions. Like Scott, Amory Blaine, the novel's main character, was an aspiring writer who attended Princeton. Unlike Scott, Amory actually served in France, but his entry into advertising following the war again reflected Scott's experience. Affairs with a series of women brought Amory no satisfaction and at age twenty-four, almost Scott's age, he realized that his over-blown ego and self-centeredness prevented him from ever being happy. As with many of Scott's later works his first novel predicted his own condition.

Scott became so excited about *This Side of Paradise* that he wrote to Maxwell Perkins, the editor who had liked his earlier work. Scott assured Perkins that he would buy this new effort, hoping that it could appear in print by October. When he did take a break from writing, he often visited a young priest, Father Joe Barron. He enjoyed their lively conversation about current events but rarely chose to discuss religion. Father Joe had a curiosity about life that Scott found attractive. He was concerned about Scott's lack of religious faith and told Scott he felt he was wasting his life.

Scott's novel was his faith. He told Bunny Wilson that he could never return to the Church. When Wilson asked Scott to contribute to a collection of stories that he was editing about the war, Scott's response was not kind. He told Wilson that he should stop wasting his energies working as an editor and write a novel instead. Wilson replied pointedly that he was writing quite a bit "and getting some of it accepted." He told Scott that his letter "looks like the attempt of a child of six." Scott ignored the criticism and sent his novel to Scribners on September 3.

For a brief time Scott took a railroad job. When told

to wear work clothes, he appeared in dirty white slacks and a white sweater, rather than the overalls most of the men wore. He would not work for the railroad long.

On September 16, 1919, he received a special delivery message from Perkins. Scribners was going to publish *This Side of Paradise*. Scott wrote back and begged Perkins to publish the novel by December. He immediately went to work on more short stories, and several were accepted by *Smart Set* and *Scribners* magazine. His work caught the attention of a well-known editor and critic at *Smart Set* named H.L. Mencken. Scott focused on having a story accepted by the *Saturday Evening Post*, the best paying magazine in the country. He signed with a literary agent in New York named Paul Revere Reynolds. Most important to Scott, Zelda now agreed to marry him.

Scott sold his first story to the *Saturday Evening Post*. Now he could afford to live well. He returned to New York and moved into a hotel, the Knickerbocker, that fit the image of the up-and-coming artist. There he gained a reputation as a drinker and partygoer. Following one party with friends he tucked twenty-dollar and ten-dollar bills into each pocket, taking care to make them hang out so that everyone could see them. His friends talked him into giving most of the cash to the hotel cashier for safe keeping before they went out. Scott returned to find the hotel authorities furious over his having left the water running and flooding his room.

Scott returned to St. Paul for Christmas, where he

Editor Maxwell Perkins would work with Scott Fitzgerald for the duration of his career. Perkins also edited the works of Ernest Hemingway, Thomas Wolfe, and other important American writers. *(Library of Congress)*

enjoyed a few parties, but stayed home to write during some of the bigger balls. His friends telephoned to explain all that he had missed. They told him of one well-known citizen who crashed a party dressed as half of a camel—he had convinced a taxi driver to assume duties as the rear half. After investigating the facts Scott began a story based on the incident. The story went into the mail the next day and the *Saturday Evening Post* bought "The Camel's Back" for $500.00. Despite his delight at the check, Scott began to experience the conflict that would haunt him throughout his career. He was torn between writing what was considered well-crafted, serious literature, and turning out the popular stories that did not challenge his talent but paid well. His need for cash was always in conflict with his desire for a literary reputation as a "serious" writer.

Scott's career continued in full swing, with the *Post* selling Hollywood agents the rights to make movies based on several of his stories. In January of 1920, Scott traveled to New Orleans in search of a new place in which to write. He visited Zelda in Montgomery and presented her with a $2,500 diamond and platinum watch, purchased with money from the sale of movie rights to a story. He also gave her an expensive, fashionable fan that he could not have dreamed of buying only a few months before. They planned their wedding, which was scheduled for after the publication of *This Side of Paradise*.

Mrs. Sayre had accepted Scott as a future son-in-law

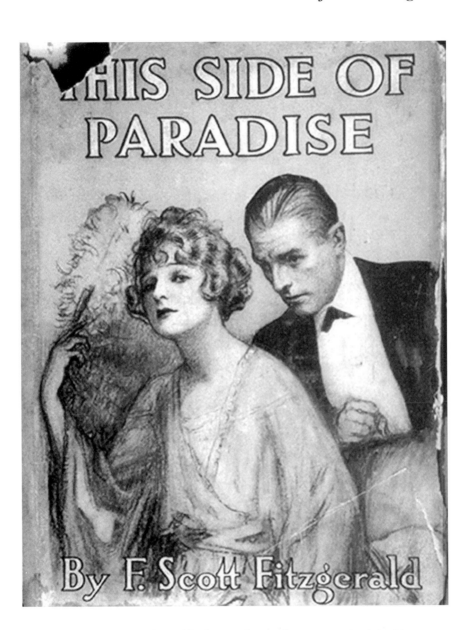

This Side of Paradise, Fitzgerald's first novel, was a huge success that helped to set the mood of the Roaring Twenties.

and wrote to him with some advice about getting along with Zelda. She warned that Zelda was "not amiable and she is given to yelping." She then told Scott that when that happened he should "give her your sweetest smile" and "go quietly about your business" until he heard Zelda begin to hum her favorite song. That meant that all was right in her world once again. Scott accepted the advice and the fact that Zelda was a headstrong young woman. Too much in love to see her erratic behavior as a warning of later problems, he eagerly tried to please Zelda.

This Side of Paradise was published on March 26, 1920 and was an immediate hit. Scott began what would become a tradition when he inscribed dozens of copies of his novel with personal notes. He then distributed them to people he admired.

Zelda sent Scott a note saying that they would soon marry and live happily ever after, like the prince and princess that Scott referred to so often. She spent her final night in Montgomery with a friend, planning to do things such as slide down stair banisters in New York in order to attract attention. Although no longer a practicing Catholic, Scott married Zelda at St. Patrick's Cathedral on April 3, 1920, but only after he sent Zelda shopping. He requested that she buy clothes a bit more tasteful than the feathers and frills that she loved.

The newly successful author and his glamorous wife soon embarked on a life together that made them one of the most famous couples of the "Roaring Twenties."

Scott helped to keep their name in the limelight by chronicling their misadventures in stories for popular "slick" magazines such as the *Saturday Evening Post.* He became the authority on the crazy parties, dances, and freer social rules of the era.

Although the scenes in his novel depicting drunkenness and "necking" between lovers shocked readers in 1920, and helped to sell copies, *This Side of Paradise* did have its critics. The reviewer in the *New York Tribune* said that Scott was like many other college-age men who pretended to have experience in sex. He felt that Scott could not accurately depict many of the emotions in the novel because he had not yet experienced them.

Despite the few negative reviews, Scott was now one of the most successful authors in America. He enjoyed the fame, and he and Zelda did a great deal to keep their reputations as a wild couple alive. During April they visited Princeton, supposedly to chaperone several parties. Scott bragged that the two stayed drunk for a week, causing the biggest disturbance ever seen at the school. He told everyone that Zelda was his mistress, and she was seen turning cartwheels down one of the town's main streets. She also poured whiskey over everyone's breakfast eggs and then lit the alcohol on fire. On the following weekend Scott created more trouble along with his old writing friends Bunny Wilson and John Peale Bishop. He visited a social group he had belonged to during his Princeton years called the Cottage Club dressed as an angel complete with a halo. He was escorted out the back door and his membership in the club was withdrawn due to his unruly behavior.

From the beginning of their marriage Scott and Zelda set a pattern of behavior that defined their relationship. At first both drank to be sociable, with Zelda sometimes simply acting the part of a drunk in order to call attention to herself. In later years Zelda stopped drinking. But Scott's drinking continued until his chronic alcoholism destroyed his marriage, career, and finally his life.

At this stage, though, they still had a great deal to learn about one another. Scott discovered that Zelda was no housekeeper. She did not care to do laundry, although he liked to change shirts several times a day. He adapted to her laziness and seemed willing to accept Zelda simply as his confidant. He confessed to a number of friends that he based some of his stories directly on Zelda's ideas. One acquaintance warned that Scott fashioned all of his female characters after Zelda and that he would soon run out of ideas. A case in point was Scott's story "The Ice Palace," published in the May 22, 1920, issue of the *Saturday Evening Post*. The first in a series of stories that compared social and cultural conventions of the South to the North, Scott focused on the influence Southern culture had on its young women. His pampered heroine, Sally Carrol Happer, an obvious reflection of Zelda, could not adjust to the cold northern climate and faster-paced life of the North when she moved to be with her boyfriend. Others observed that

Zelda interrupted Scott's work. She was both his inspiration and his distraction. While Zelda seemed to accept the role of advisor-to-the-artist, she would later challenge Scott's right to incorporate her ideas and phrases into his stories.

But for the time, the two proved inseparable, like a team of entertainers, set on disrupting life for everyone. The couple's antics became legendary. They purposely remained quiet during the funny scenes at the movies, then laughed loudly during the serious parts. Scott stood on his head in the lobby of the Biltmore Hotel, claiming he had to do something outrageous because he had not seen his name in the papers that day. When the Biltmore asked the Fitzgeralds to leave after several weeks, they spent some time at the Commodore Hotel, but eventually rented a house in Westport, Connecticut.

As much as Scott's childish behavior may have irritated some, his fellow writers found him gracious with his time and energies. He willingly helped other writers, offering editing suggestions for their manuscripts. He also found time to write. During the summer of 1920, he began a novel that would become *The Beautiful and the Damned*.

Late in the summer Scott and Zelda decided to make a quick trip to Montgomery to visit her friends and family. The trip almost ended in tragedy. While there Scott became jealous of all the attention given to Zelda. He felt irritated that Zelda's pampered childhood left

her unprepared and unwilling to take care of the sim-
plest of household chores. Washing dishes, mending
clothing, and making up beds were simply not in Zelda's
sphere of experience. During the visit it became clear
to him that Southern ladies from Zelda's social position
expected special treatment. At the same time, Zelda
resented the fact that Scott did not want her to buy
many of the luxuries she wanted. The pressure grew
during the trip until their pent-up frustrations erupted
into a public argument. Zelda took an earlier train and
arrived in New York before Scott. When she went to the
station to meet him, his train almost ran over her as she
walked on the tracks. Scott himself had acted irrespon-
sibly by boarding the train with no money to pay for his
ticket. The quarrel that erupted in the railroad station
remained a point of contention for the next twenty
years.

In September of 1920, Scribners published Scott's
first collection of short stories, *Flappers and Philosophers*. Some critics felt it did not fulfill the promise of
Scott's novel. They called the stories "slick" and "com-
mercial," and said they lacked literary style. In his
stories, written for the high-paying magazines, Scott
created charming, cocky characters that behaved the
way he would like to behave: with perfect freedom to
indulge in irresponsibility. Although few people like
those characters actually existed, they still came to
represent the era for their readers.

Chapter Five

Roaring into the Twenties

Scott continued friendships with Edmund Wilson and John Peale Bishop. Both men worked as editors at *Vanity Fair* magazine and both were surprised by Scott's success. Although they considered him a friend they did not take him seriously as a literary figure. They thought his style was "light," and both men considered themselves to be more talented artists. Bishop had his first book of poetry published in 1920 and was not happy that Scott's novel gained so much of the praise, publicity, and profits for that year. Scott revealed his own lack of confidence by looking to more veteran editors, such as H.L. Mencken and George Jean Nathan, co-editors of the *Smart Set* magazine, for advice and praise.

Scott worked on *The Beautiful and the Damned* during April of 1921. Zelda suggested a change in the conclusion, and Scott's editor agreed. Scott made the revision. However, Scott and his editor disagreed on a

Editor George Jean Nathan published Scott's best stories in *Smart Set. (Library of Congress)*

few issues. One was the shabby treatment of the Old Testament in his story. His editor felt that the plot showed a lack of respect for the Bible. In the end, the editor won, and Scott softened his treatment.

In the spring of 1921, Zelda announced that she was pregnant, and the two decided to vacation in Europe. Before they could leave, Zelda persuaded Scott, who was already quite drunk, to pick a fight with a bar bouncer several times his size. They had to postpone sailing for Europe until Scott's injuries healed. They left a week later and visited England and Paris and took a tour of Italy that lasted several months. While the couple delighted in visiting Europe's high society attractions, they did not seem to notice that many countries continued to struggle to recover from the devastation of World War I. Their own good fortune blinded them to the depressed conditions of much of the world. When the couple returned to the United States they talked mainly about the future birth of their baby. They decided they wanted the child to be born in St. Paul.

Scott came home to Minnesota as the triumphant author. Zelda delivered their daughter, Frances Scott Fitzgerald, whom they nicknamed Scottie, on October 26, 1921. Scott insisted that his daughter be baptized into the Catholic Church, even though a friend overheard him muttering shortly before her birth, "God damn the Catholic Church, God damn God."

Zelda and Scott called their daughter "Scottie." *(Library of Congress)*

As Scott told those who were interested, his last time to attend confession had been in the service while he was stationed in Montgomery, and he only did it then because his date wanted him to accompany her.

The Fitzgeralds quickly grew bored with St. Paul's quiet life. Scott became critical of his parents. He exaggerated their personalities to others, depicting his father as attractive but unimportant, and his mother as a woman who lacked style. Scott's friends thought that he did not seem to know where his fiction ended and reality began.

Scott was not pleased with the cover art for his new novel. However, he was very pleased by the public's reaction when *The Beautiful and the Damned* appeared on March 3, 1922. Mencken congratulated him for writing something different from his first novel. Nathan thought it first rate, and Wilson thought it was a great improvement over *This Side of Paradise*. The couple in the novel, Anthony and Gloria, clearly represented aspects of Scott and Zelda, although they were not meant to be identical. Anthony's main goal in life was to end up with his grandfather's money, money he had not earned himself, but felt he deserved. By the end of the novel, Gloria had lost her good looks and Anthony had become a hopeless alcoholic. The ruin suffered by the fictional couple was prophetic of the Fitzgeralds's own future.

For the time being, however, nothing threatened Scott's success. His goal was to become the best writer of his generation and to live on his writing income. In March 1922, the Fitzgeralds visited New York City, where Scott intended to continue his climb toward that goal. He began work on another short story collection, maintaining Scribners' policy of releasing a volume of his short stories following publication of a novel.

While in St. Paul, Scott graciously agreed to write a show for the Junior League for free. He could not afford to do too many such favors, as his four most recent stories did not generate enough income to support the family and he refused to moderate his lifestyle. He had borrowed $5,643 from Scribners, in anticipation of wide sales of *The Beautiful and the Damned*. However, the novel's sales proved disappointing, despite its critical acclaim. Where Scott had predicted sales of 60,000 copies, only 43,000 were sold.

Despite the need for income, Scott turned down a Hollywood offer. A studio wanted to make a movie version of *This Side of Paradise*, and the executives wanted Scott and Zelda to play the main roles. When Scott refused, Perkins was relieved. Scott focused instead on writing a play that he predicted would be "a sure-fire money-maker." On September 22, 1922, Scribners released his story collection *Tales of the Jazz Age*. Many of the tales featured characters enjoying a wild lifestyle that included uncontrolled spending and wasting of their time and energies. In October the Fitzgeralds moved back to New York, where Scott hoped to find a producer for his play.

Scott became friends with writer Ring Lardner. *(Library of Congress)*

Scott and Zelda rented a house on Great Neck, Long Island, the location that he later used as the setting for his novel *The Great Gatsby*. They lived in the house for two years, with occasional trips to Europe. Scott and Zelda were happy in New York. He wrote to a friend about Scottie: "We dazzle her exquisite eyes with gold pieces in the hopes that she'll marry a millionaire."

During this time Scott became friends with another up-and-coming American writer, Ring Lardner. The two became close confidants and often went out drinking together.

Zelda and Scott were a celebrated pair. Invitations to their parties were highly sought after. However, those invited often arrived to find total chaos. The food might not appear until hours later than expected, or one dish might appear, but not another. Sometimes the so-called guest of honor did not even attend. On one such occasion guests were told the party would honor a writer named Rebecca West, but she never arrived. Scott painted a face on a pillow, topped it with a hat, and placed it in the chair intended for West. Always the entertainer, he drank throughout dinner while insulting the pillow. Guests later learned that the invitation had been extended to West at the last moment, and she could not find the house, due to poor directions. In addition to his antics and practical jokes, Scott became known for his pet phrases. For a time, he constantly applied the term "knock-out" to people and objects and later termed everything an "egg," good or bad. One guest referred to Scott as "the doom of youth itself."

Scott fell into a daily routine of working, drinking, then making the party rounds. Although they met many people, the Fitzgeralds had few close friends due to their unpredictable and often undesirable behavior. One night Zelda invited guests to a candlelight supper. A woman who had been making advances toward Scott

Scott and Zelda became notorious for their flamboyant behavior. *(Library of Congress)*

appeared at the door. Although Scott sent the woman away, he and Zelda argued. Scott jerked the tablecloth from the table, sending china and glass smashing to the floor. He once hit a policeman dressed in plain clothes who he felt had insulted Zelda. A newspaper headline read, "Fitzgerald Knocks Officer This Side of Paradise." Depending on his mood and how much gin he had consumed, Scott would either valiantly defend Zelda's honor or insult her in public.

Although Scott complained about devoting so much time to magazine stories, he had little choice. A story such as "The Popular Girl," quickly completed in the week of Scottie's birth, sold to the *Saturday Evening*

Post for $1500. When time allowed, he also produced higher quality stories, such as "The Diamond as Big as the Ritz," which only brought in $300 from *Smart Set*, a journal with a reputation for publishing fine literature. His problem was excessive spending. During 1920 Scott's income was $18,500, an amount roughly equal to $110,000 at the end of the twentieth century.

Scott's play, a farce called *The Vegetable,* appeared on stage in Atlantic City on November 20, 1923. An audience that included the mayor enjoyed the first act, but the later acts confused them. Even Scott left the theater, along with Zelda and the Lardners, to visit a nearby bar before the play concluded. He worked for a week to try to repair the play before giving up.

The sale of movie rights to *This Side of Paradise* earned $10,000, none of which he saved. He always thought he could make more money but rarely had money available to pay the bills. Following the failure of his play, he had to work hard for the next several weeks writing stories to pay the expenses. Although he showed admirable self-discipline when financially pressured, such concentrated effort resulted in various physical problems, including stomach aches and sleeplessness, which tended to lead to more drinking.

As they stayed on in Great Neck, the Fitzgeralds' drinking caused their behavior to turn destructive. Scott would disappear for days at a time while Zelda worried. Once he turned up asleep on a neighbor's lawn. At other times he would involve Zelda in his tricks. Just for fun, the couple once drove their car into a pond while entertaining Mr. and Mrs. Maxwell Perkins. The Fitzgeralds had to climb out and push the car onto dry land. Scott bought expensive jewelry for Zelda that she sometimes threw away while angry. Both became more emotionally unstable. Scott's instability was due mostly to his drinking, but it slowly become clear that Zelda's problems had existed for years. While others began to suspect that she was mentally and emotionally ill, Scott seemed to ignore Zelda's symptoms.

In April of 1924 the Fitzgeralds traveled to France, a new "hot spot" for the trendy members of the American social scene. The sudden wealth of the twenties produced among some a sense of self-centered security and independence. Many accepted their new wealth as a permanent condition. Scott envied this attitude and sense of security. He desperately desired the life of the decadent rich, but he did not have the flow of funds to support it and, most critically, had the true artist's awareness of the transitory nature of life. He could never be totally contented.

While not immune to the trends of the era he helped to create, Scott had his own more private reasons for traveling to France. First, he knew that he and Zelda could live more cheaply there; like much of Europe, France still suffered from the destruction and debt caused by World War I and had a low cost of living. Second, despite his desire for instant wealth and fame, Scott also longed for the permanence the written word allowed. He hoped that leaving the distractions of home would help him to write seriously. Other artists, not caught up in the glamour of the era, had already elected to live abroad. Disillusioned and emotionally shattered by the destruction of World War I, these American artists, called "expatriates," would become highly influential in the arts in the decades to come. An expatriate herself, the American writer Gertrude Stein dubbed the expatriates "The Lost Generation."

In Paris, the Fitzgeralds soon became part of the group that gathered around the wealthy Americans Gerald and Sara Murphy. The Murphys introduced the Fitzgeralds to other writers and artists. They spoke of a young writer they had met named Ernest Hemingway. The Murphys were convinced Hemingway was the best American writer in Paris. The Murphys enchanted the Fitzgeralds with their stories about the wonders of the French Riviera, the coast of France along the Mediterranean Sea. Soon Scott and Zelda left for the South of France, traveling from Paris through Normandy, Lyon, Dijon, and Avignon to arrive in Provence. There they took up residence in St. Raphael, a town Zelda described as having "an air of repressed carnival about it." Although they had planned to economize, they hired a nanny for Scottie and happily took up residence in the beautiful area.

Scott settled down to work seriously on a new novel. He had started work on *The Great Gatsby* while they still lived in Great Neck, but was having trouble making progress. Zelda spent hours swimming and soon complained of being bored. She began spending time on the beach with a young French aviator named Edouard Jozan. Scott did not appear to be jealous, as he had seen many men flirt with Zelda, until she began to spend almost all her time with Jozan. Although no one knows for certain that Zelda had a love affair with Jozan, there were ru-

Scott and Scottie on the beach in 1925.
(Library of Congress)

mors that she asked Scott for a divorce after confessing to the affair. In one journal entry he referred to "The Big Crisis–13th of July," but did not identify that crisis. Zelda later referred to that time in a letter to Scott when she wrote, "then there was Josen and you were justifiably angry."

While no one may ever know for certain what happened between Scott and Zelda during the summer of 1924, it is worth noting that he was writing a novel with sexual infidelity as a major plot point. In *The Great Gatsby,* tragedy consumes the hero because of his efforts to win a wife, who was more than a little reminiscent of Zelda, away from her husband.

The Fitzgeralds continued their bizarre behavior. Returning home from Nice later that summer, they decided to drive along the train tracks rather than follow the road. When the car stalled, they both fell asleep and might have been hit by the morning train had a passing worker not roused them.

All was clearly not well. Then, one morning in September of 1924, Scott, pale and upset, awakened the Murphys. Zelda had taken an overdose of sleeping pills. No one determined whether Zelda's act was a suicide attempt or an accident.

Despite the chaos of his life, Scott continued to work on his novel until he finished it that fall. After sending the manuscript to Maxwell Perkins, and copies to several of his friends, the family spent the winter of 1924-1925 in Rome, where he revised the novel and wrote short stories. One, titled "The Sensible Thing," appeared on July 15, 1924, in the magazine *Liberty*. It focused on George O'Kelly, a young man who loses his love, only to recapture her devotion again at a later time. He realizes, however, that he can never recapture the original passion of their romance. Scott concludes the story with George thinking: "April is over, April is over. There are all kinds of love in the world, but never the same love twice." The story may reflect Scott's own experience of winning Zelda back following their broken engagement, or it may be charged by the aftermath of her possible adultery of the previous summer.

Scott's stories continued to appear in the *Saturday*

Evening Post, bringing $2500 each, five times the amount earned by his first story. He told Perkins that the more the pay, the less he could stand to write such "trash." Another important event occurred in the fall of 1924: Scott met Ernest Hemingway. In a letter to Perkins in October he urged his editor to read Hemingway's newly published book of short stories entitled *In Our Time*, published the previous March. This was the first of hundreds of such references in Scott's letters.

Chapter Six

The Price of Fame

The Great Gatsby was published in April 1925 to great critical praise. Scott's most valued review came from H.L. Mencken. Scott had written in the copy of *Gatsby* that he mailed to Mencken, "I'd rather have you like a book of mine than anyone in America." Mencken wrote to tell Scott that the new book was his best work yet. Other writers who agreed with Mencken's assessment included American authors Willa Cather and Gertrude Stein.

It was clear to all who followed his work that this novel was a giant step forward from Scott's first two novels. While the earlier works had been energetic and refreshing, they lacked the sustained, coherent vision and the subtle, flexible style of *The Great Gatsby*.

Despite the high praise from critics and other writers, the novel sold fewer than 23,000 copies, far below Scott's expectations. Although he knew he had extended his talents and written a novel that he was proud of, he wrote to Perkins that if his next novel did not generate more money, he was going to move to Hollywood and learn the movie business. He could not bear the insecurity caused by a lack of income. He acknowledged that he lived beyond his means, but he felt incapable of doing anything about it. "I had my chance back in 1920 to start my life on a sensible scale and I lost it and so I'll have to pay the penalty."

Scott began to spend more time with Ernest Hemingway, whom he greatly admired. Their relationship would become legendary. The two men were different in many ways. Where Scott was slight and rather delicate, Hemingway was robust and athletic. Where Scott's prose was free-flowing, romantic, and impressionistic, Hemingway's was restrained, clear, and understated. Having driven an ambulance in Italy for the Red Cross during World War I, where he was severely wounded, Hemingway wrote knowingly of war-time hospitals and disillusioned soldiers coming home. Scott continued to be obsessed with wealth and how it separated people in American society.

Despite their seeming differences, each recognized the other as a serious artist and had a deep respect for the other's talent. Hemingway, a favorite of Gertrude Stein, took Scott with him to call on her. Stein's apartment was a meeting place for artists and writers in Paris. Stein was an experimental writer who encouraged new writers to break with tradition.

Another of Scott's visits did not go as well. In July of

1925, Scott received a written invitation to visit the famous American author Edith Wharton, whom Scott had admired for years. From a wealthy family, Wharton entertained in the high tradition. Guests were expected to deport themselves with impeccable manners. Scott was accompanied on his visit by a friend who knew Wharton, too. Nervous about meeting Wharton, Scott had several drinks. He ended up telling a vulgar story to his hostess and her guests and was then whisked away by his embarrassed friend. Wharton wrote the single word "Horrible" in her diary beside Scott's name.

After the publication of *The Great Gatsby*, Scott's alcoholism grew worse. He continued to do childish things while drunk. Even the Murphys grew tired of his antics. During one drive into Paris, Scott chewed up and spit pieces of hundred franc notes (roughly equal to twenty dollar bills) out of a taxi cab window. When the driver stopped to gather the money, Scott jumped behind the wheel and drove recklessly toward the Seine River. Murphy stopped him, allowing the driver who had chased them on foot to reclaim his taxi. On another occasion Scott pretended to pass out in a drunken stupor and fell to the floor. He wanted Gerald Murphy to pick him up, but Murphy told Scott, "this is *not* Princeton and I am *not* your roommate. Get up!" Scott did as ordered. Although Scott had promised Perkins another novel by October, the month passed without much work completed. The less he wrote, the more he drank; the more he drank, the less he wrote.

Scott would become lifelong friends with writer Ernest Hemingway.
(Library of Congress)

The Fitzgeralds visited London in November, then returned to Paris in December. Zelda, who was complaining of a lack of energy, decided to take a "cure" in Switzerland. A short time later, they moved back to the French Riviera, where Scott seemed more enthusiastic about his writing than he had for months. He had begun a new novel, *Tender is the Night*, and his third collection of short stories, *All the Sad Young Men*, had been published and was selling well. In addition, *Gatsby* had been adapted into a successful play on Broadway, and the movie rights had sold. This brought Scott badly needed income. The money allowed him to avoid writing the bothersome quick-sale short stories for more than a year.

He was not able to remain focused on his work for long, however. In June of 1926, they traveled to Paris where Zelda underwent surgery for an intestinal problem. Once she recovered they began another round of drinking in bars and crashing parties. Their friends noticed that Scott and Zelda sometimes seemed to be locked in an intense, destructive competition over which one could exhibit the worst behavior. At home they argued long and often. Their public misbehavior seemed to relieve pent-up frustration on both of their parts. Scott was frustrated at the amount and the quality of the work he was getting done, and Zelda felt that she had been pigeon-holed as the wife of a famous writer.

Scott did not have to be with Zelda to create a drunken scene. After arguing with one bar buddy about whether a man could actually be sawed in half, Scott and a friend tied a bartender across two chairs. When Scott's friend left to find a saw, the bartender yelled loudly enough to bring the police. Scott based a scene in his next novel, *Tender is the Night*, on the incident.

Friends observed that Zelda's actions had become stranger than ever. She was often like a hunter waiting to verbally attack people. Once she lay down in front of a car and begged Scott to run over her. Scott meanwhile attended a party at the Murphys' and was evicted from the premises for three weeks for throwing a frozen fig at the bare back of a countess and destroying three of the Murphys' favorite goblets by pitching them over a wall into the street. Promptly at the end of three weeks he reappeared at his friends' front door, assuming the friendship would continue. His charm convinced the Murphys to forgive him, but he did most of his drinking thereafter in bars with Hemingway.

By December of 1926, Scott and Zelda were ready to go home. They had decided to travel to Hollywood, where Scott would work on movie scripts to bring in the money they needed to support their ostentatious lifestyle. When they booked passage on a ship, Scott wrote to Perkins to inform him that he still had not finished the novel. One of their fellow passengers, Ludlow Fowler, had been best man at their wedding and was himself newly wed. Zelda took Ludlow aside to tell him that if he desired a good marriage he should not let alcohol take over his life.

The Fitzgeralds rented a home in Hollywood, and as 1927 began, Scott started work on a script for a movie called *Lipstick*, which was supposed to be a light-hearted movie about flappers and boys at Princeton, but was never filmed. He also began a romance with young Hollywood starlet named Lois Moran. At seventeen, she was a little more than half of Scott's age, but he was captivated by her flawless French, sophisticated charm and lovely looks. Lois had grown up in Paris, where she danced with the ballet. Now she was in Hollywood with her mother. The two satisfied one another's romantic interests in an idealistic way. Lois wanted Scott to play a leading male role in a movie, something he knew better than to take on. Scott later used Lois as a model for his character Rosemary Hoyt in *Tender is the Night*.

While Scott worked on the doomed movie script, Zelda found life in Hollywood to be dull. Although she worried about Scott's drinking, she did her part to help him liven up their own parties. During one gathering, guests decided to investigate a strange smell coming from the kitchen. They found Scott dropping the ladies' handbags into the cooking tomato sauce.

Scott received an advance payment of $3,500 from the United Artists studio for the *Lipstick* script and would have been paid another $12,500 if the movie had been completed. His plan to make money in the movies had come up empty. He spent more money in California than he earned.

The Fitzgeralds relocated to a large house near

Wilmington, Delaware, in March of 1927. Scott planned to concentrate on his novel, but the quiet life did not satisfy him or Zelda. Once more they threw legendary parties from which everyone emerged exhausted. Novelist John Dos Passos wrote, "Those delirious parties of theirs; one dreaded going. At Wilmington, for instance, dinner was never served. Oh, a complete mess . . . a wild time."

Lois wrote Scott from Hollywood: "I miss you enormously—Life is exceedingly dull out here now." She also thanked him for sending her a copy of Hemingway's recently published, highly successful novel, *The Sun Also Rises*. The book featured a hero, Jake Barnes, who was quite different from any that Scott created. Barnes had been rendered impotent in the war and lived in Paris among the "Lost Generation," where he struggled against the self-indulgence and decadence that Scott's heroes, and Scott himself, embraced.

Scott and Hemingway regularly read and reviewed one another's manuscripts. Hemingway wrote in April to ask, "How is your novel? Have you finished it? When is it coming out?" But Scott did not work much that summer. His quarrels with Zelda became more frequent and more consuming, and his drinking continued. Zelda also drank too much and required medication. Her physician hoped a morphine shot would settle her "hysteria" over Scott's remarks about her lack of a profession.

Scott returned to Princeton in September of 1927 for the first time since being kicked out of the Cottage

Club in 1920. *College Humor* had asked Scott to write a piece about his alma mater. He renewed his love of football as he watched several team practices. The Cottage Club invited Scott to speak, and he showed up sober, but when he stood before the group, no words came. He made several efforts to begin before someone told a vulgar joke to pass the time. Then the gathering dissolved into a round of story-telling. An embarrassed Scott later drank too much at a local party.

That fall, while Scott was in New York, H. L. Mencken and an assistant visited him at his hotel. When Scott told them the story for a new novel that included a suicidal heroine, Mencken remarked that he just described Zelda. Scott became furious, and later Mencken told his assistant that Scott would amount to little unless he got rid of Zelda. They only saw her increasingly outrageous public behavior and what seemed to be unrealistic demands for Scott's money and attention. They did not see how much she had served as an inspiration for his work.

What was clear was that Scott lacked confidence. In a November 1927 letter, Scott praised Hemingway's recent short story collection *Men Without Women*. Despite the congratulatory tone, Scott's jealousy toward Hemingway was evident when he reminded his friend that the *Post* paid him $3,500 per story. The vast differences in the personalities of the two men was also clear in a December letter from Perkins to Scott. He mentioned having sent Hemingway a $1,000 check and that

Editor H. L. Mencken commented that Scott would never succeed unless he left Zelda.
(Courtesy of the Library of Congress.)

Hemingway, who had not expected it, responded that he might not spend it because "he finds he lives according to the amount he has, however little it may be." Such a phrase could never be applied to Fitzgerald.

Despite Scott's insecurities, inability to work, and alcoholism, the Fitzgeralds did share some pleasant times as a family. The Christmas of 1927, Scott and Zelda bought a dollhouse for Scottie and worked together to build, paint, and furnish it, an activity Zelda particularly enjoyed. Scottie was delighted with her gift and with the many stories her father told her.

In February of the following year, Scott's old friend Edmund Wilson attended a Fitzgerald party that he described in an article. Wilson was by now a highly respected editor and critic who worked at the *New Republic*, a prestigious magazine. He had not seen Scott since 1924 but still thought of him fondly. Having behaved wildly himself in his past, "Bunny" accepted Scott back into his circle. They would occasionally go out together with another friend, Gilbert Seldes. The nights out gave Scott time away from Zelda, although Zelda resented his absence.

Scott had lost confidence in his future and thought his talents were in decline. He also became much less optimistic about America's future. This pessimism was becoming more prevalent as the 1920s headed toward a close. Americans had the general feeling that the country took its resources for granted, and many thought that it was only a matter of time before the country would collapse from a lack of values. On the surface the United States appeared to prosper, but not everyone enjoyed the new-found wealth. Factory workers and farmers struggled with low wages and prices for their goods. In some ways, Scott was the representative man of the 1920s. His early income promised success, but his short-sighted attitude toward money did not allow him to plan for his future. Many other Americans had made the same mistake. Scott did nothing to alter his behavior, but it seemed that this new insight sapped his energy and took much of the joy out of writing. It was almost as though his genius was born and died with the era.

Scott struggled to be productive. He later admitted that is was during this time that he first began to drink to stimulate his creativity. He was mining the deeper regions of his life and talent for the new novel, more so than in the previous books.

Again desperate to reinvigorate their marriage and Scott's talent, the couple decided on yet another relocation. This time they moved back to Paris, in the spring of 1928. Scott hurried to write some short stories to pay for the trip.

Chapter Seven

Zelda's Descent

In Paris, Zelda's behavior became increasingly bizarre. In restaurants she would request foods that were difficult to find, embarrassing others in the party. If members of her group were enjoying themselves, she would break-up the fun by demanding to be taken home. When she complained that Scott ignored her, he spent more and more time with his drinking friends. Sylvia Beach, a bookstore owner and writer friend, wrote about Scott and Zelda in her book *Shakespeare and Company*: "Poor Scott was earning so much money from his books that he and Zelda had to drink a great deal of champagne in Montmarte in an effort to get rid of it." Tensions between the two continued to grow, even though Scott told others that he learned everything that he knew about life from his wife.

But Zelda did not want to exist simply as a character inside another person's art. She wanted to have a career of her own. She published a few stories, began painting, and then, in another of her strange decisions, decided to take up dancing, an activity she had loved as a child. At the time she was twenty-eight, an age when most ballet dancers are thinking of retirement. Zelda invited the Murphys to the dance studio where she practiced. Gerald Murphy later described her dancing as "really terrible," adding, "one held one's breath until it was over." He speculated that Zelda was trying to hold onto her youth, commenting, "there's nothing worse; it ruins a woman." One benefit of the dancing was that she and Scott argued less, but their anger was replaced by silent suspicion.

The Fitzgeralds returned to Delaware in September of 1928. When his thirty-second birthday rolled around in September, Scott commented that he had made no progress on the work that mattered to him, although he had earned an impressive $30,000 that year. He also stated that he had wrecked others as well as himself. Zelda continued with dance lessons in Philadelphia and spent hours practicing at home. She ignored Scott and worked out before a huge mirror that he thought looked like a fixture from a brothel. Zelda loudly proclaimed her hate for the chauffeur that had come to America with them from France. He served as Scott's drinking and boxing partner, an activity that Scott had picked up from Hemingway. Zelda complained that Scott's boxing and drinking cut into time he could spend with Scottie. She wrote that Scott offered little in the way of parental guidance.

During the winter of 1928-29, Zelda wrote the first of six short stories that focused on the lives of six different young women. *College Humor* had previously published two of Zelda's articles and its editors agreed to accept five stories. However, they insisted on publishing the stories under both Zelda's and Scott's names, to assure sales. Zelda continued to push herself hard, practicing her dancing for hours, then exerting more energy on her stories. As she and Scott grew further apart she accused him of having a homosexual affair with Hemingway.

When their lease ended in 1929, the Fitzgeralds left again for Europe. Scott wrote to Perkins in March of 1929, "I am sneaking away like a thief without leaving the chapters." He asked that Maxwell trust him "a few months longer" and told him he would "never forget your kindness and the fact that you've never reproached me."

When they arrived in Paris, Zelda immediately resumed her ballet lessons with her former teacher. Scott was usually out drinking when she arrived at home in the evenings. When they were together the two irritated one another more than ever. Part of the tension was due to Zelda's dislike of Hemingway, a feeling that he returned. He told Scott that when he first met Zelda he thought her crazy. In *A Moveable Feast*, a book of memoirs about his years in Paris, published in 1964 after both authors' deaths, Hemingway wrote, "I did not know Zelda yet, and so I did not know the terrible odds that were against him. But we were to find them out soon enough."

Hemingway and Scott's friendship had cooled, although they still enjoyed an occasional drink. Hemingway had divorced and remarried in 1927, and he was working hard to complete a new novel about World War I called *A Farewell To Arms*. Hemingway had little sympathy with Scott's lack of self-discipline and angered Scott by refusing to listen to him complain about his unfinished novel.

An informal boxing match between Hemingway and a sparring partner in June of 1929 almost ended their relationship. Although conflicting stories emerged about the event, Scott apparently let the round clock run too long and exposed Hemingway to injury. Scott was drunk at the time and while Hemingway was understandably frustrated, he was not actually angry over Scott's inattentiveness. What provoked him were Scott's continuous claims of innocence, as if Hemingway had accused him of something he had nothing to do with. For the next several months Hemingway and Scott separately corresponded with Perkins about the event, but they did not speak of it to one another for some time.

The Fitzgeralds traveled to the Riviera in the summer of 1929. During the visit, the Murphys noticed that Zelda was pale and haggard. She frequently burst into laughter for no reason and distanced herself from family and friends. Scott had a deathly, unhealthy pallor and suffered from nervous attacks. He frequently quarreled with the Murphys. At summer's end he wrote to Hemingway that he felt he had not a friend in the world. Although they had argued a month earlier, Hemingway was sympathetic. He urged Scott to try to shake his depression, adding that he bet the novel was actually good. Hemingway told Scott that when he was drunk and felt he had no friends, he should remember "Ernest the stinking serial king." Hemingway used the term "serial" to refer to his books, which often appeared a chapter at a time in magazines before the complete version was published.

Despite the encouragement, Scott did not work on his novel. His income from 1929 reflected his focus on magazine stories. He earned $27,000 for eight *Saturday Evening Post* stories and $31.71 in book sale royalties. Scott's income was enviable, although it was still not enough to support his opulent lifestyle.

In September of 1929, one month before the crash of the United States stock market, Zelda received an invitation to join the ballet school of the San Carlo Opera Ballet Company of Naples, Italy. She did not accept the invitation and Scott never mentioned it when he spoke of her dance career. He continued to deal with the aftermath of the sparring incident with Hemingway. An error-filled report about the boxing match, written by a person who was not present, appeared in the *New York Herald Tribune* in November, fanning the flames of the smoldering disagreement. It took several correspondences through the rest of the year before both men understood that neither of them had been responsible for the story. In a December 1929 letter Hemingway assured Scott that he knew him to be "the soul of honor."

Still living in Paris in 1930, after the stock market crash of October 1929, Scott and Zelda decided to visit North Africa in February. They wanted to escape the social whirl and the pressure of their disintegrating relationship. Upon their return to Paris, Zelda had become more paranoid. She worried that others gossiped behind her back. Her ballet teacher noticed that she seemed less able to concentrate.

Finally, in April of 1930, Zelda suffered a nervous breakdown. Scott admitted her to a hospital outside Paris, where she paced her room anxiously. She expressed concern that she would not be allowed to write or dance while at the clinic. The doctors described her condition as anxiety complicated by exhaustion from dancing. After only two weeks, Zelda checked out, although her doctors felt she was not yet ready to leave. She returned to her ballet and had a second break down at the end of May. This time she checked into the Valmont Clinic in Switzerland.

After two weeks Zelda's physicians could see that she required in-depth psychiatric treatment. A psychotherapist named Oscar Forel diagnosed her as a schizophrenic who lived in a fantasy world. Her symptoms included seeing people and objects and hearing voices that did not exist. She was transferred to a sanitarium in Prangins, near Geneva, Switzerland. In June she wrote to Scott and pleaded with him to speak to her dance instructor to find out whether she truly had a future as a dancer. She also asked Scott to remove her from the clinic. She concluded by writing, "Every day it gets harder to think or live and I do not understand the object of wasting the dregs of me here, alone in a devastating bitterness." For years Scott had refused to acknowledge Zelda's fragile mental state. Now he had no choice.

For the next year Scott wandered around Switzerland, staying close to Zelda. After visits with Scottie in Paris he always returned to Prangins. While in Paris, he remained in contact with various writers. He met writer Thomas Wolfe, famous for his novel *Look Homeward Angel*.

For a time Scott hoped that some physical condition would be found to explain Zelda's problems. She remained nervous, breaking out in rashes when she learned that Scott planned a visit. When Dr. Forel told Scott that he needed to stay away, Scott ordered flowers sent to Zelda every other day and asked permission to send notes that did not mention her illness. Soon after Zelda entered Prangins, Scott inquired of Perkins whether Scribners might be interested in publishing several stories that Zelda wrote while in the hospital. Scribners declined and the stories were later lost.

Throughout June and July of 1930, Zelda swung from an apparent normal state to near-hysteria. She saw Scottie in August but still did not want to see Scott.

Scott blamed Zelda's mother for having been too pro-
tective of her as a child. Still, he had to assume some
responsibility, especially when Dr. Forel instructed him
not to drink for a year. The doctor explained that Zelda
wasted energy she did not have to spare worrying about
Scott's alcoholism. He then informed Scott that Zelda
had only a one in four chance of completely recover-
ing.

Chapter Eight

Things Fall Apart

Scott furiously wrote stories to pay for the best treatment for Zelda. He had not touched his novel in months. He wished he could do more serious work, but his friends had little patience with his complaints. In fall of 1929, Hemingway had written that Scott used his "juice to write for the *Post*," leaving him only the "dregs" to use in writing his novel.

In May of 1930, Scott had been pleased to hear from his old friend Shane Leslie, who invited him to visit London. Leslie also expressed his sympathy for Zelda's illness. By that summer she had improved, no longer laughing at the wrong moments or breaking out in hives. Her love for Scott even resurfaced. In an August letter she called him "the best" and added "O my love, I love you so—and I want you to be happy."

While abroad Scott had put much effort into correspondence with friends and business associates, but he rarely wrote to his parents. His mother, despite her devotion, irritated him, although he still loved his father. Scott returned to St. Paul when his father died in January 1931. He stayed for the funeral, then visited Zelda's family in Montgomery, before returning to be close to Zelda in Prangins. In September 1931, following one year and three months of treatment, Zelda left the sanitarium. Scott planned to spend the winter in Montgomery. He thought that Zelda could enjoy her childhood surroundings while he finally returned to work on the novel.

When Scott brought Zelda back to the States they passed through New York City. He noticed how much life had changed in America. Little of the gaiety from the 1920s remained; many people had lost everything. Many speculators had borrowed to invest in the stock market and had lost not only their investments but still had large debts to repay. Many could no longer purchase goods they had bought freely before and manufacturers had warehouses of products with no customers. Unemployment sky-rocketed, mills and factories closed, and many farmers could not sell their goods to the world market because the rest of the world followed the United States into depression.

The depression seemed to have hardly affected Montgomery, Alabama, because there had never been much wealth there at any time. Scott wrote to Perkins that life was simple there and he intended to work hard. Scott maintained an optimistic attitude, even regarding his relationship with Zelda. Although her acquaintances expressed shock at how she had changed, Scott was never heard to complain about Zelda's illness. Instead, he tried to build her confidence by praising her in front of others.

In October 1931, Scott returned to Hollywood where he was offered $1,200 per week from MGM Studios to work on a script. The script failed, but Scott was well-received by members of the Hollywood community. The producer who rejected Scott's script, Irving Thalberg, became fond of Scott. He believed that artists who achieved fame would always hold their talent. Norma Shearer, a famous actor and Thalberg's wife, met Scott at their party. Although he got drunk and embarrassed himself and the guests by singing a childish song he had written at Princeton called "Dog! Dog! Dog!" he received a telegram the following day from Norma Shearer that read, "I thought you were one of the most agreeable persons at our tea." Scott would later base the heroine and hero from his last, unfinished novel, *The Last Tycoon*, on the Thalbergs.

While Scott was away in California, Zelda wrote expressing concern about his being around such beautiful women. She filled her letters with loving phrases and discussed Scottie's school and activities. She even felt kinder toward Hemingway, suggesting to Scott that they reduce their cost of living and practice the economic approach used by Ernest.

In November Judge Sayre died. His loss greatly affected Zelda. Scott came home for the funeral and took

Zelda to Florida afterward, where she had an asthma attack. A few days later she suffered a relapse of her mental illness. Scott placed her in the Phipps Clinic in Baltimore, Maryland, and then returned to Montgomery. In February of 1932, Zelda wrote, "think of me—if my room is as empty to you as yours was when you were away you will find yourself living in an ether dream— as if there was a veil between you and reality." Zelda's illness had kept Scott writing stories, and 1931 brought his highest income yet: $37,599. However, he had turned out stories so rapidly that even the editors at the *Post* complained of their decreased quality.

Zelda soon showed signs of recovery. She relaxed at the clinic and wrote and painted. She began work on a novel, *Save Me the Waltz*, that dismayed Scott by incorporating personal details from their lives. He argued with her about it but she continued writing the book her way. When she finally cut some scenes, Scott felt better. He had another reason, relating to Hemingway, to be hesitant about Zelda publishing her book. According to Scott, Ernest had declared that he never wanted to publish a book the same year as Scott. Scott feared Ernest also did not want to publish the same year as Zelda. Scott wrote to Maxwell Perkins and advised him not to praise Zelda's novel to Hemingway.

Scribners accepted Zelda's novel in March of 1932, and she progressed quickly. Scott moved to Baltimore to be near her. In May he rented a house on a small estate known as La Paix in the Maryland countryside.

His arrival attracted attention in the normally quiet country area. A long line of cars and vans delivered Scott's furniture and personal items, as well as Scottie and her French governess. He then turned, at last, to serious work on his novel.

Scott did take time out from his work for trips to Princeton football games. He made friends with his landlord's family, the Turnbulls, and even took eleven-year-old Andrew Turnbull along with him to a game. He convinced Mr. Bayard Turnbull to set aside room for a tennis court, where he invited Andrew to play with Scottie, who was the same age. Spur-of-the-moment boxing matches in a circle of grass marked off as a ring were not unusual. Scott enjoyed organizing games for the children. Andrew later wrote about chatting with Scott, dressed in his bathrobe, on the porch after a day of writing.

As for his novel, Scott ended up rejecting his original idea for a book to be titled *The World's Fair*. He had planned to base the novel on the 1924 kidnapping and murder of a child of wealthy Chicago socialites. His plot, featuring the murder of a mother by her son, had caused him problems from the beginning. As with his other novels, Scott had chosen to interweave characters and plot lines based on events in his own life. He would still do that with his new novel, but it would not be based on the murder case. He would write about himself and Zelda: How the world can challenge a great artist, and the spiritual death to which that challenge can lead.

That summer of 1932 Perkins wrote to Hemingway. He shared his hope that Zelda would become a popular author in order to relieve the financial pressure on Scott. Hemingway wrote back that Scott should have "swapped" Zelda several years previous, before her insanity surfaced. He called Scott "the great tragedy of talent in our bloody generation." Later that day, Ernest sent a telegram to Perkins, apologizing for his harsh words. He explained that the Fitzgerald marriage and its negative effects on Scott had always angered him.

Meanwhile, Zelda seemed to improve. She spent time with her family, returning to the clinic only occasionally. Visitors observed her dancing on the lawn at La Paix as the wind-up Victrola played a favorite record. She swam with Scottie, then soaked up the sun on the bank or on a floating raft as she smoked. She also rode horses and started writing a play. People who observed Scott and Zelda together thought them a loving couple, but the strain between them still existed.

Scott had to enter the hospital for two weeks that summer. At first his doctor thought he had typhoid fever, but it turned out that he needed rest due to nervous exhaustion. Perkins visited Scott later and wrote to Hemingway, "Scott did not look so well, but he was in fine spirits, and talked a lot." He also told of Scott's wanting to spend the afternoon drinking. Despite his drinking, Scott continued working. He wrote in his journal that the novel would "never more" be "permanently interrupted."

Zelda liked her new doctor, Thomas Rennie, who had begun to work on her case along with Dr. Adolf Meyer. Dr. Rennie had at one time wanted to be a writer and found the Fitzgeralds interesting. He worked to keep Zelda on a schedule of early morning writing, exercise before lunch, and painting in the afternoon. But Scott's drinking increased the tension between the two, and Zelda had to resist the urge to fight with him at night when he was drunk. Dr. Rennie took a call from Zelda on August 29, 1932. She demanded that he place her in a clinic called Sheppard-Pratt for treatment of nerves. After telling Zelda that her best hope was to remain out of the hospital, Dr. Rennie asked both Scott and Zelda to visit him together.

Dr. Rennie explained that the Fitzgeralds faced three different causes of conflict. The first was the competition with one another caused by their artistic careers. The second was Zelda's effort to simultaneously be a mother and a wife, while also fulfilling her career. The third problem centered on their sexual relationship. Although both had idealistic views of marriage, neither worked hard to meet the physical needs of the other. Scott admitted to being the weaker of the two, then said that Zelda had looked for support from stronger men during their marriage. He claimed to be on the verge of a breakdown and accused Zelda of trying to take advantage of his nervousness. Dr. Rennie asked that they all look forward to the publication of Zelda's novel, hoping that would help resolve the conflict.

Save Me the Waltz was published in October, 1932, but it was not a success—ending both Dr. Rennie's and Maxwell Perkins's hopes that the book would take pressure off of Scott. The Fitzgeralds's popularity did not generate interest in the novel, and not all of the three thousand printed copies sold. Reviewers were unkind regarding Zelda's style, and Hemingway described the book to Perkins as "unreadable."

Meanwhile, Scott made good progress on his own novel. Once again parallels to Scott's relationship with Zelda were obvious in the book's plot. Its main character, a brilliant psychiatrist named Dick Diver, meets his future wife, Nicole, when he cares for her as a mental patient. After she recovers through his therapy, they marry. He ends up sacrificing his promising career while fulfilling his wife's desires.

In January 1933, Scott met his old friend Edmund Wilson, along with Hemingway, in New York City. All three later agreed their time together was spoiled because of Scott's drinking. According to Wilson, Scott lay his head on the restaurant table during the meal and threw up in the bathroom. Although Hemingway warned Scott to stop teasing people, Scott managed to insult both of his friends. Before departing, Hemingway told Scott that Zelda's problems should not interfere with his writing, hinting that Scott would be a coward if he used her illness as his excuse for not getting more work done. Wilson accompanied Scott back to his hotel and tried to talk with him, but Scott became more difficult.

Scott's record of the get-together concluded that "strong" individuals should only discuss polite subjects. He later told Perkins, "I write with the authority of failure—Ernest with the authority of success. We could never sit across the table again."

Chapter Nine

Life Goes On

Scott regularly corresponded with Zelda's psychiatrist. In April 1933, Scott asked whether the doctor should not tell Zelda how she exhausted everyone's patience. When Dr. Meyer identified Scott's alcoholism as part of Zelda's problems, Scott explained that the doctor only heard Zelda's views. Scott still believed he needed to drink to write, claiming that he did not drink for pleasure but in order to reach his potential.

In May Dr. Rennie joined the Fitzgeralds at La Paix for a taped interview. Scott blamed Zelda for his unfinished novel. He explained that he had lost three years due to "a sickness" and five more because Zelda "wanted to be a ballet dancer; I backed her in that." Zelda argued that Scott's drinking caused her to long to escape through dancing "because I had nothing else." Later, Scott told Zelda that he felt alone in his "struggle" against other "gifted" writers, while she was "a third rate writer and a third rate ballet dancer." As he began to speak of having "dominated" the writing field, Zelda broke in and commented, "It seems to me you are making a rather violent attack on a third rate talent." Zelda, no longer a bright, confident socialite, obviously needed far more from Scott, a man in conflict over his career, than he could give. While both wanted to understand the other's weaknesses, neither was capable.

Despite his problems with Zelda, Scott continued to shape his novel. He referred to it in a letter as "my phantom novel which is now really in its last stages." Sacrificing all other writing, he neared completion. He hoped that the public had not forgotten him and the novel would be a success.

Life at La Paix soon developed into more of a routine than Scott had known in years. His life became more quiet and subdued in the country. The Turnbulls became accustomed to seeing Scott always in his pajamas, regardless of the hour. He invited them over for dinner on July 4, 1933. He enjoyed discussing books with Mrs. Turnbull and loaned her his copy of Thomas Wolfe's *Look Homeward Angel,* a book that sought to capture the suffering of a sensitive youth, much as Scott's earlier work had done. After hearing the news that the wife of the Turnbulls's gardener was sick, he asked about her health. When she died, he visited the gardener's home during the wake. There he knelt beside the coffin, a coat covering his pajamas. Although Scott was not religious, the act was something he believed might bring comfort to the family.

Although busy with his novel, Scott took time out to play with Scottie, Andrew Turnbull and his two sisters, Eleanor and Frances. He doted on Eleanor, who, in Scott's opinion, had a future on the stage or screen. Scott even wrote a play for Scottie and Eleanor to act before the Turnbull family. Andrew Turnbull later explained that he and Eleanor saw Scott as a combination of magician and inventor.

Zelda slipped further into mental illness as Scott grew even closer to his daughter. Several of his short stories had themes of fatherhood, including the powerful story "Babylon Revisited." This story focused on the struggle of a reformed alcoholic to reclaim custody of his daughter following his wife's death, for which others held him responsible. Although unflinching in revealing the damage the alcoholic father had done, the story ended with a sign of hope that he would recover.

Although Scott was generous and loving with Scottie, he also had expectations. He wanted her to do well at sports and languages, and he expected perfect manners and high morals from her. When Scott discovered a box kept outside by Scottie and Eleanor used to exchange messages about sex, he punished Scottie. He told her that she could not contact Eleanor for seven days. On other occasions Scott made promises, then broke them, in order to teach Scottie "character."

From the relative calm of his life at La Paix, Scott knew that the world had changed. He mourned the passing of the Jazz Age. Watching Zelda's condition worsen increased his sense of loss. During her visits to La Paix, Zelda often sat for long hours outside, while Scott encouraged her to play tennis and swim with Scottie. In June he ended a letter to Zelda by writing, "I believe however you are not giving it, giving us, a fair trial here. If I didn't love you so much, your moods wouldn't affect me so deeply."

During the second year at La Paix the Turnbulls detected a change in Scott. His drinking began to escalate and he spent less time in social activities. He saved most of his energy for the novel. He now received much less pay from the *Post* for stories, and, for the first time, he complained to Zelda about the expense of her care. In June 1933, Zelda burned something in an unused fireplace on the second floor of La Paix and the house caught on fire. When the firemen arrived they kept the flames from spreading to the first floor. Scott handed out drinks to all who came to watch the fire. Despite damage to the house, he asked Mr. Turnbull not to repair it, as the construction noise would distract him. He continued to work on his novel while surrounded by water-damaged walls.

Scott appointed John Peale Bishop to be his "literary executor" in August of 1933. This meant that should he die or become incapacitated, his friend would have control over all of his writings, including the nearly-finished novel. Scott could not decide on a title for the book, which was scheduled to be published in serial form in *Scribners* magazine beginning in January 1934.

The serial would be followed by the book publication later that spring. He wrote to one friend that he planned to name the book for its main character, *Richard Driver*, if no better title came to mind. By November, however, the title had been decided. Scott chose *Tender is the Night* from a line taken from the English romantic poet John Keats's famous poem "Ode to a Nightingale."

Scott wanted Hemingway to like his book. Because Hemingway had been on a hunting safari in Africa from December of 1933 until February 1934, Scott did not speak with him before the novel went to press. Perkins wrote to Hemingway that he felt the new book would allow Scott to regain his prominence as a novelist. As Scott nervously looked forward to the publication, he had to deal with Zelda's third major nervous breakdown in January of 1934. She moved into Sheppard-Pratt Hospital outside of Baltimore and visited La Paix when she could.

As chapters of the novel appeared in *Scribners*, Scott began to hear from friends and critics. He felt bolstered by comments such as that from Thomas Wolfe, who wrote that the book was Scott's best, and from John Peale Bishop, who told Scott, "It surpasses *The Great Gatsby* [. . .] you are a true, a beautiful and a tragic novelist." Poet Archibald MacLeish wrote, "Great God, Scott you can write. You can write better than ever. You are a fine writer. Believe it. Believe It—not me." However, Hemingway wrote to Perkins on April 30 that he had read Scott's book, "and it has all the brilliance and most of the defects he always has. In spite of marvelous places there is something wrong with it." He later added, "The trouble is that he wouldn't learn his trade and he won't be honest. He is always the brilliant young gentleman writer, fallen gentleman writer, gent in the gutter, gent ruined, but never a man." He concluded by asking Perkins not to show the letter to Scott.

Scott helped to arrange an exhibit of Zelda's paintings in New York City in 1934. The paintings were offered for sale from March into April. Magazines that reviewed the art show dedicated more page space to reviewing Zelda's past than to discussing her work. *Time* magazine did describe her work as that of a "brilliant introvert," labeling it "vividly painted." The article concluded by saying that Zelda hoped "her pictures would gratify her great ambition—to earn her own living." However, not many paintings sold and Zelda was disappointed by the public's reception of her art.

Scott wrote to Hemingway and asked his opinion of *Tender is the Night*. Ernest replied that he liked some of it. He then urged Scott not to worry about creating bestsellers when he wrote, but to present his stories realistically and to forget his personal problems. He added, "I'd like to see you and talk about things with you sober," and "I'm damned fond of you." Scott's reply in June showed that Hemingway had hurt him, but his tone remained calm.

Tender Is the Night sold only 15,000 copies. Sales did not even bring in enough money to repay the cash

Poet Archibald MacLeish praised Scott's novel *Tender is the Night*.
(Library of Congress)

Scott had borrowed from Scribners to live on as he completed the novel. Disappointed by the sales, Scott spent much of the remainder of 1934 isolated at La Paix, although he encouraged Scottie, then almost thirteen years old, to socialize. He wrote several small pieces, some of which did not even sell. He hoped to sell a movie version of *Tender is the Night*, but no one bought the script.

Toward the end of May 1935, Zelda became more confused. When she told her doctors that Scott terrified her, he stopped visiting. Devastated by Zelda's condition, Scott searched for a project that might help her come to terms with life. He designed a three-part book for her to work on. The first part was to be titled, "Eight Women." The suggestion did revive Zelda and she began planning the cover design—but the revival did not last. Scott began to see her again and during one visit Zelda ran toward the train tracks close to the clinic, determined to throw herself under a train. Scott chased and caught her before she could carry out her plan. She spoke of suicide often.

Scott had to earn some money. Although he had released a collection of stories, *Taps at Reveille*, in 1935, he had little income. He decided to write a series of letters that dealt with personal matters to be published in *Esquire* magazine. He would be paid the magazine's "going rate" of $250 per article. Scott submitted a total of eleven pieces that appeared between 1934-1936. The first one, "Show Mr. and Mrs. F. to

Number___," bore Scott's and Zelda's names as co-authors. All of his pieces were "confessionals," articles in which he discussed personal issues dealing with the writing life, particularly his feelings of disappointment, exhaustion, and failure.

At the same time Hemingway was also writing for *Esquire*. The two authors' works could not have been more different. Hemingway wrote of sporting expeditions and also published two of his most famous short stories, "The Snows of Kilimanjaro" and "The Capital of the World," in the magazine. Hemingway made a negative comment about Scott in "The Snows of Kilimanjaro" that offended him, but Scott's admiration of his old friend's talent remained firm. Scott continued his contributions, which became known as the "crack-up" essays. They took that name from the title of one of the pieces in which Scott described his marriage and career falling apart. He knew that Hemingway and others felt that he had lowered himself to a shameful level by revealing such intimate parts of his life for money, but he felt he had no choice. The pay he received for a story had fallen from $4,000 to only $250.

Chapter Ten

The Death of an Idealist

From March through June of 1935, Perkins sent Hemingway several "bulletins" announcing that Scott had "gone on the wagon," ending his drinking. For most people this would mean not touching any alcohol. For Scott, not quite thirty-nine years old, it meant that he only drank beer, not hard liquor.

Scott left Baltimore to visit Asheville, North Carolina, where he hoped to rest. Charmed by the beautiful, mountainous countryside, he decided to move there permanently. Zelda's condition worsened; she believed that she had conversations with Jesus Christ and several historical figures. Scott asked that she be dismissed from Sheppard-Pratt. He planned to move her close to his new residence. On April 8, 1936, Scott delivered Zelda to Highland Hospital in Asheville. He worked with Zelda's new doctor, Dr. Robert Carroll, to give her occasional releases to visit him and her mother. He could no longer deal with Zelda full time, but he wanted to give her every chance for a possible recovery. He told friends that he knew that, were conditions reversed, she would do the same for him.

Zelda continued taking brief trips, and her mother pushed to have her released to her care. Scott tried hard to control his anger over the Sayres's repeated insistence that Zelda be released. He was convinced Zelda should never live outside an institution again. He spoke of Zelda, who was only thirty-six years old at the time, as his invalid, but never lost sight of all that she had been to him. Over the years Scott had occasional affairs with women, but he likened them to his drinking—they provided an escape from reality.

When his mother died in September of 1936, Scott accepted one more loss in the best way that he could. Mollie Fitzgerald left $47,000 to Scott and his sister, Annabel. After paying back to her estate the money Scott had borrowed from his mother, he inherited $17,000. Scott focused his attentions on Scottie, telling friends that she provided a reason for him to live.

Facing constant illness brought on by stress and alcoholism, Scott felt sure that he would die young. He refused to stop drinking, even during the times when he required a live-in nurse. After embarrassing Scottie with his drunken behavior at a 1936 Christmas party, he checked into a hospital and in the spring of 1937 managed to stop drinking altogether for a while. His only hope for steady income seemed to be Hollywood, and he would have to be sober to do script work. Scott checked out of the clinic, living quietly while waiting for his long-time agent, Harold Ober, to negotiate a contract to work on movies. He had gained seventeen pounds and felt stronger when word came that he had a contract with MGM studios to work for $1,000 per week. This meant one year's worth of guaranteed income. He owed Ober $12,500 for services and almost that much to Perkins.

On June 4, 1937, Scott listened to Hemingway deliver a speech to a prestigious New York City club. They spent a brief time together. Afterwards their careers would take them in totally different directions. While Hemingway continued to produce novels, and later won the Nobel Prize for Literature, Scott hoped that Hollywood would provide for his future.

Scott told his friends that he would work hard while charming the movie community. When Scott arrived, those who remembered his earlier visits found his appearance shocking. The alcohol had taken an enormous physical and emotional toll. His new co-workers, however, liked Scott. They described him as surprisingly humble and willing to learn.

A few days after he arrived in California in the summer of that year, Scott met twenty-eight year old Sheila Graham, an ambitious journalist who wrote newspaper columns about people and events in Hollywood. Born into poverty in the East End of London, Graham had created a false background for herself as an educated British woman from the upper class. Soon she and Scott were lovers, and she would be his on-again, off-again companion for the rest of his life.

Most of the time the couple avoided the social scene. When they did attend parties Scott seemed to hang in the background. Neither were drinking at that point, although several months into their relationship, Scott went on a binge that horrified Sheila. She committed herself to fighting his alcoholism and many people credited her with lengthening Scott's life.

By October 1937 the movie work did not seem nearly as exciting. Scott did not enjoy writing scripts based on other people's novels. He told Harold Ober that he wished to write an original script. He especially disliked co-writing with others. Eventually, Scott found a project that he did like. He would help write a script version of a novel by the German novelist, Erich Maria Remarque. He hoped to receive a "credit," meaning his name would appear on the movie screen.

The studio renewed Scott's contract for twelve months at $1250 per week, but in January 1938 the movie's producer cut most of Scott's contribution to the script. When he wrote to Harold Ober, he did not even try to hide his bitter disappointment.

Occasionally, Scott left Hollywood to take Zelda on short trips. At the end of March 1938, Scottie accompanied them to Virginia Beach. Scott began to drink during the trip and Zelda reacted by telling everyone in the hotel that he was a maniac. The trip convinced him that he could never again help Zelda, and he returned to

Hollywood. Sheila talked him into renting a bungalow together on Malibu Beach. Scott did not enjoy swimming and spent little time on the beach because of his fair skin. They did enjoy cooking exotic meals together.

Scottie was set to graduate from her Connecticut boarding school in June, and Zelda wanted to attend the ceremony. Her doctor agreed to let her go, providing a nurse would accompany her part of the way. Following graduation Zelda returned to the hospital and Scottie stayed on campus to take her college exams. A short time later Scottie broke the campus rules by leaving without permission. When school authorities asked her to move off campus as punishment, Scott was furious. Not long after, however, they learned that Scottie scored high on her exams and that she had been accepted to Vassar College for the fall. Scott was so pleased that he financed a European trip for Scottie to celebrate.

Scott had made an effort to make a success of Hollywood and to control his drinking. But into his second year of working for the movies he expressed his unhappiness to several friends. He told Maxwell Perkins, "I thought it would be so easy, but it's a disappointment." He described Hollywood as "barren," adding, "I don't *feel* anything out here." His next projects were unsuccessful, and in December the studio did not renew his contract. Scott wrote to friends that he actually felt some relief. He had begun to suffer sweats and a recurrent fever and he feared that he had tuberculosis. He had spit up blood on several occasions.

Scott befriended Sheila Graham during the last years of his life.
(Library of Congress)

In February 1939, Scott was hired as co-writer for a movie project titled *Winter Carnival*. It had to be filmed on location at Dartmouth College in New Hampshire. Because he felt so ill Scott did not want to make the trip to view the campus first-hand, but the director insisted. Sheila accompanied him as far as New York City. Due to poor planning Scott had to share servant's quarters on the campus with a co-writer. He began to mourn the loss of his career, and, as all such circumstances tended to do, this led to drinking. Within days Scott was fired from the project.

Scott returned to Hollywood with Sheila, still hopeful of finding work. He left briefly during April to take Zelda on a trip to Cuba. While there he was beaten up for trying to stop a cockfight. He became ill, and the trip had to be cut short. It would be his final visit with Zelda, who moved into Highland Hospital permanently.

The previous fall Scott had moved from the beach to Encino, California. He rented a small home on the estate of Edward Everett Horton, a popular actor. He felt comfortable there and Sheila visited often. She took care of him as he spent two months in bed. An x-ray revealed a lesion on one lung, but Scott still wanted to work. He did isolated jobs for several different studios without a contract, but his poor health made it difficult for him to report to the studio everyday. Still determined to write, he turned again to magazine stories.

The debt to Harold Ober had been paid, although Scott still owed money to Perkins. He requested another

$500 loan from Ober and promised a story. Ober agreed, but he told Scott he did not want this type of relationship to become a habit. When Scott sent Ober two old stories that he had been unable to sell, he also asked for more money. After years of putting up with Scott, Ober had to refuse to advance him any more money. Scott, embarrassed and angry, ended their long relationship. He then tried to sell his stories directly to magazines. But he had lost contact with what magazines wanted, and his efforts proved largely unsuccessful.

Scott decided in the fall of 1939 to return to novel writing. *Colliers* magazine indicated that it might be interested in publishing a new book in serial form. They wanted to read 15,000 words before making a final commitment, but if the editors liked it they would advance Scott $30,000. Desperate for money Scott mailed the first 6,000 words of what would become *The Last Tycoon*. *Colliers* insisted on seeing more before sending money. Scott sent his material to the *Post* instead, but those editors also would not commit to publication. Perkins read it, thought it a good beginning, and mailed Scott $250 of his own money, telling him he would be able to send another $1000 in January. The support proved crucial to Scott, who felt that only Maxwell Perkins and his old friend Gerald Murphy had remained loyal. Murphy had loaned Scott money to pay Scottie's bills at Vassar, and Scott felt a great emotional, as well as financial, debt to him.

Sheila visited Scott often, although he became highly

possessive of her and was often difficult. They once wrestled over a gun that Scott kept loaded in case of burglars; Sheila believed it too dangerous for him to keep in the house. She also found him chatting with two homeless men whom he had picked up on Ventura Boulevard and brought to his house. When his actions became more bizarre, she decided to leave him. She refused to speak to Scott on the phone, but he mailed her threatening notes that told her to "get out of town" or "you'll be dead in 24 hours." Despite Scott's irrational behavior, the two eventually reunited.

In the spring of 1940, Scott wrote to Scottie, "I am not a great man." He added that he did, however, feel that his work had value. He spoke tearfully to his sister Annabel of his talent. Although he no longer spoke with Hemingway, he remained curious about his old friend who had done what Scott had been unable to do: hold onto his talent and fame. Sheila later wrote that Scott still admired Hemingway but would not see him again, "until after the publication of *The Last Tycoon*, and only, then, if the book was the hoped-for-success." Understanding that Scott was very ill, Sheila asked a friend to assume some of her writing duties. She also turned down a $1000 offer for a speaking engagement that would have required travel. She spent more time with Scott. She asked him to help her write some short stories, and they began what she later called a tutorial. He clearly enjoyed suggesting books for her to read and guiding her education in other ways. Scott craved friendship, and he managed to grow close again to Edmund Wilson. Scott wrote in his journal of the book he was working on: "This novel is for two people—S.F. [Scottie] at seventeen and E.W. [Edmund Wilson] at forty-five. It must please them both."

Scott continued to write although he was growing weaker. He suffered a heart attack in late November while visiting a pharmacy. After that his doctor told him not to climb stairs. Sheila invited him to take a spare room in her apartment until he could find an apartment without stairs. She occasionally became impatient with Scott. He was obviously ill, but she believed he faked an even worse condition in order to gain sympathy. She wrote, "when Scott was sober he was a hypochondriac, and I was never sure whether he was shamming or really ill."

On December 20, 1940, Scott attended a movie pre-view with Sheila to celebrate having finished a scene in his novel. When they stood to leave, he stumbled and told Sheila that he felt exactly as he had that day in the drugstore. The outside air revived him and by the next day he chatted happily about his novel and Scottie as he and Sheila waited for his doctor to visit. Scott dictated a letter for Scottie that Sheila wrote out for him. She then left for a short time to buy some candy and sandwiches. Later, after she returned, Scott decided to read a foot-ball article in the most recent *Princeton Alumni Weekly*. He told Sheila that he wanted something sweet to eat, and she offered him her candy bar. A few moments later

Scott jumped to his feet and clutched the fireplace mantle. He fell to the floor.

When she could not revive Scott, Sheila ran to a neighbor's apartment for help. The neighbor felt for Scott's pulse and lay on his chest to listen to his heart. He shook his head. The paramedics arrived and pronounced Scott dead.

Scott was buried in Rockville, Maryland on December 27, 1940. Zelda could not attend the funeral. The Murphys, Perkinses, Obers, Turnbulls, and Scottie, along with a few other friends, braved the frigid weather to attend the simple Protestant service. Although he had not practiced his religion for some time, Scott's will requested a Catholic funeral. However, due to his separation from the church, this was not allowed. He could not be buried with his ancestors.

His close friends felt devastated by the loss of such a talented and generous man. Edmund Wilson wrote to Zelda, "I know how you must feel, because I feel myself as if I had been suddenly robbed of some part of my own personality." Zelda celebrated the 1941 publication of Scott's final novel *The Last Tycoon* and wrote of Scott, "He was as spiritually generous a soul as ever was," adding, "although we weren't close any more, Scott was the best friend a person could have."

Zelda became very religious following Scott's death. Her paintings again were exhibited in 1942, to a lukewarm reception. When Scottie married Lieutenant Samuel Jackson Lanahan in New York in 1943, Zelda could not attend the wedding. The two did remain on good terms and often corresponded. During her occasional visits with Scottie, Zelda delighted in her grandchildren.

Over the next several years Zelda traveled between Highland Hospital and her mother's home in Montgomery. She wrote a letter to Scottie on March 9, 1948 from the hospital where she had begun to receive insulin treatment for diabetes. Around midnight on March 10, a fire that began in the kitchen of the hospital moved up the open shaft of the dumbwaiter to the roof, then leaped onto each hospital floor. The wooden fire escapes on the outside of the building caught fire and there was no internal sprinkler system. Although hospital staff and firemen attempted to rescue the patients, many of them had locked their doors, and their windows had been chained shut. Nine women, Zelda among them, died. A charred slipper beneath her body was used for identification.

Zelda Sayre Fitzgerald was buried next to Francis Scott Key Fitzgerald on a bright, unseasonably warm St. Patrick's Day, March 17, 1948. Mrs. Turnbull, one of several friends and mourners, brought two pansy wreathes to the cemetery. After the service, she carefully placed them side by side, one on each of the Fitzgeralds's graves.

Fitzgerald's Legacy

Although he had not been totally forgotten at the time of his death, the majority of the reading public thought of F. Scott Fitzgerald as a writer who had never lived up to his promise. The uncompleted *Last Tycoon* was published in 1941, and gained some critical praise, but it seemed that Fitzgerald's reputation as a writer was an artifact of the 1920s, as dated as bath tub gin and goldfish swallowing. Then, in 1945, his friend Edmund Wilson, who had often been critical of his work while he was alive, edited the essays Fitzgerald had written for *Esquire* and published them in a volume titled *The Crack Up*. The same year, a collection of his fiction, called *The Portable Fitzgerald,* was published and a reappraisal of his work began. By the end of the 1950s, Fitzgerald was almost universally respected as a writer of serious fiction.

The Great Gatsby, which had been dropped from the Book of the Month Club in the 1930s because of slow sales, was selling 300,000 copies a year by 1980, and both that novel and *The Last Tycoon* had been made into major movies. Fitzgerald's works are now read and taught in classes around the world, and his novels and stories of doomed idealism, the ruthlessness of social classes, and the destruction that can result from "the pursuit of happiness," may be the best fiction ever written about these essential American themes.

Sources

CHAPTER ONE—Born to Write

p. 11, "I have drawn a prize in a wife." Andrew Turnbull, *Scott Fitzgerald* (New York: Scribners, 1974), 5.

p. 12, "started then to be a writer." Ibid.

p. 15, "third in her affections . . ." Ibid., 15.

p. 15, "Dear God, . . ." Ibid., 15-16.

p. 19, "fortunate," and "I must excell, even in the eyes of others . . ." Ibid., 33.

p. 21, "as slender and keen and romantic . . ." Ibid., 41.

CHAPTER TWO—Writing, College and Romance

p. 22, "ADMITTED SEND FOOTBALL PADS AND SHOES IMMEDIATELY PLEASE WAIT TRUNK." Turnbull, *Fitzgerald*, 44.

p. 24, "What sort of . . ." Ibid., 50.

p. 27, "In your conversation . . ." Bruccoli, Matthew J., and Margaret M. Duggan, eds. *Correspondence of F. Scott Fitzgerald* (New York: Random House, 1980), 15-16.

p. 30, "poor boys shouldn't . . ." Turnbull, *Fitzgerald*, 73.

CHAPTER THREE—Zelda

p. 31, "I had read somewhere . . ." Turnbull, *Fitzgerald*, 76.

p. 33, "first rate stuff," Bruccoli and Duggan, *Correspondence*, 21.

p. 33, "I wish you would stick to . . ." Ibid., 22.

p. 38, "someday recreate . . ." Turnbull, *Fitzgerald*, 93.

p. 38, "Sweetheart . . ." Nancy Milford, *Zelda: A Biography* (New York: Harper and Row, 1970), 39.

p. 39, "EVERYTHING IS POSSIBLE . . ." Turnbull, *Fitzgerald*, 93.

p. 39, "love to fancy themselves . . ." Milford, *Zelda*, 44.

p. 40, "they locked princesses in towers . . . if it's going to be . . ." Bruccoli and Duggan, *Correspondence*, 43.

p. 40, "Old death . . ." Milford, *Zelda*, 46.

CHAPTER FOUR—Birth of a Professional

p. 41, "haunted . . . my drab room . . ." Turnbull, *Fitzgerald*, 98.

p. 43, "and getting some of it . . ." Ibid., 101.

p. 48, "not amiable and . . ." Ibid., 107.

CHAPTER FIVE—Roaring into the Twenties

p. 55, "God damn the Catholic church . . ." Sara Mayfield, *Exiles from Paradise: Zelda and Scott Fitzgerald* (New York: Dell, 1971), 74-75.

p. 57, "a sure-fire money-maker" Turnbull, *Fitzgerald*, 137.

p. 57, "We dazzle her . . ." Ibid., 137.

p. 58, "the doom of youth itself." Ibid., 141.

p. 59, "Fitzgerald Knocks . . ." Ibid., 144.

p. 62, "an air of repressed carnival . . ." Milford, *Zelda*, 106.

p. 63, "The Big Crisis . . ." Ibid., 110.

p. 63, "Then there was Josen . . ." Bruccoli and Duggan, *Correspondence*, 246.

p. 64, "April is over . . ." F. Scott Fitzgerald, " 'The Sensible Thing.' " *The Short Stories of F. Scott Fitzgerald*. Matthew J. Bruccoli, editor (New York: Scribners, 1989), 301.

CHAPTER SIX—The Price of Fame

p. 66, "I'd rather have you . . ." Carl Bode, editor. *The New Mencken Letters* (New York: The Dial Press, 1977), 139.

p. 67, "I had my chance . . ." Turnbull, *Fitzgerald*, 166.

p. 68, "Horrible." Ibid., 159

p. 68, "this is *not* Princeton . . ." Ibid., 166.

p. 73, "Those delirious parties . . ." Milford, *Zelda*, 132.

p. 73, "I miss you . . ." Bruccoli and Duggan, *Correspondence*, 206.

p. 73, "How is your novel? . . ." Matthew J. Bruccoli, *Fitzgerald and Hemingway: a Dangerous Friendship* (New York: Carroll & Graf, 1984), 87.

p. 75, "he finds he lives . . ." Ibid., 211.

CHAPTER SEVEN—Zelda's Descent

p. 78, "Poor Scott was earning . . ." Sylvia Beach, *Shakespeare and Company* (New York: Harcourt, Brace and Company, 1956),116.

p. 79, "really terrible . . . one held one's breath," Milford, *Zelda*, pp. 141-142.

p. 80, "I am sneaking . . ." Andrew Turnbull, *The Letters of F. Scott Fitzgerald* (New York: Scribners, 1971), 217.

p. 80, "I did not know Zelda yet . . ." Ernest Hemingway, *A Moveable Feast* (New York: Charles Scribner's Sons, 1964), 176.

p. 82, "Ernest the stinking . . ." Ibid., 135.

p. 83, "the soul of honor." Bruccoli, *Dangerous Friendship*, 148.

p. 84, "Every day it gets harder . . ." Bruccoli and Duggan, *Correspondence*, 237.

CHAPTER EIGHT—Things Fall Apart

p. 86, "juice to write . . ." Bruccoli, *Dangerous Friendships*, 132.

p. 86, "the best" and "O my love," Bruccoli and Duggan, *Correspondence*, 267.

p. 88, "I thought . . ." Ibid., 282.

p. 89, "think of me . . ." Ibid., 283.

p. 91, "swapped," and "the great tragedy . . ." Bruccoli, *Dangerous Friendship*, 161.

p. 91, "Scott did not look . . ." and "never more . . ." Milford, *Zelda*, 260

p. 93, "unreadable" Ibid., 161.

p. 94, "strong" Bruccoli, *Dangerous Friendship*, 163.

p. 94, "I write with . . ." Ibid., 165.

CHAPTER NINE—Life Goes On

p. 95, "a sickness . . ." Milford, *Zelda*, 273.

p. 96, "my phantom novel . . ." Bruccoli and Duggan, *Correspondence*, 315.

p. 98, "I believe however . . ." Ibid., 313.

p. 99, "It surpasses . . ." Ibid., 339.

p. 99, "Great God," Ibid., 323.

p. 99, "and it has all the brilliance . . ." Bruccoli, *Dangerous Friendship*, 166-67.

p. 100, "brilliant introvert . . ." Milford, *Zelda*, 291.

p. 100, "I'd like to see . . ." Ibid., 172.

CHAPTER TEN—The Death of an Idealist

p. 108, "I thought it would be . . ." Turnbull, *Fitzgerald*, 301.

p. 112, "get out of town . . ." Ibid., 314.

p. 112, "I am not . . ." Ibid., 314.

p. 112, "until after . . ." Sheila Graham, *The Real F. Scott Fitzgerald: Thirty-five Years Later* (New York: Grosset & Dunlap, Inc., 1976), 208.

p. 113, "This novel is for . . ." Turnbull, *Fitzgerald*, 322.

p. 113, "when Scott . . ." Graham, *Real Fitzgerald*, 212.

p. 114, "I know how you must feel . . ." Milford, *Zelda*, 350.

p. 114, "He was as spiritually . . ." Turnbull, *Fitzgerald*, 332.

Major Works

Bibliography

Baker, Carlos, ed. *Ernest Hemingway: Selected Letters, 1917-1961.* New York: Charles Scribner's Sons, 1981.

Beach, Sylvia. *Shakespeare and Company.* New York: Harcourt, Brace, & Co., 1959.

Bode, Carl. *The New Mencken Letters.* New York: The Dial Press, 1977.

Bruccoli, Matthew J. *Fitzgerald and Hemingway: A Dangerous Friendship.* New York: Carroll & Graf, 1994.

Bruccoli, Matthew J., and Margaret M. Duggan, eds. *Correspondence of F. Scott Fitzgerald.* New York: Random House, 1980.

Fitzgerald, F. Scott. " 'The Sensible Thing.' " *The Short Stories of F. Scott Fitzgerald.* Editor Matthew J. Bruccoli. New York: Scribners, 1989. 289-301.

Graham, Sheila. *The Real F. Scott Fitzgerald: Thirty-five Years Later.* New York: Grossett & Dunlap, 1976.

Hemingway, Ernest. *A Moveable Feast.* New York: Charles Scribner's Sons, 1964.

Mayfield, Sara. *Exiles from Paradise: Zelda and Scott Fitzgerald.* New York: Dell, 1971.

Milford, Nancy. *Zelda: A Biography.* New York: Harper & Row, 1970.

Turnbull, Andrew. *The Letters of F. Scott Fitzgerald.* New York: Scribners, 1971.
───. *Scott Fitzgerald.* New York: Scribners, 1974.

Websites

The 1920s—A comprehensive site devoted to the Roaring Twenties
www.louisville.edu/~kprayb01/1920s.html

F. Scott Fitzgerald Centenary—Univ. of South Carolina
www.sc.edu/fitzgerald/

Scott and Zelda Fitzgerald Museum
www.alabamatravel.org/central/szfm.html

Index